A NEW DESIGN FOR LIVING

Ernest Holmes
and
Willis H. Kinnear

PRENTICE
HALL
PRESS

New York   London   Toronto   Sydney   Tokyo   Singapore

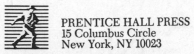 PRENTICE HALL PRESS
15 Columbus Circle
New York, NY 10023

Library of Congress Catalog Card Number 90-50816

ISBN 0-13-615592-8

Manufactured in the United States of America

13 12 11 10 9 8

THIS BOOK IS DEDICATED TO THOSE WHO
WOULD DISCOVER WITHIN THEMSELVES THAT
MORE WONDERFUL PERSON THEY MAY BECOME

*Wisdom is the principal thing; therefore get
wisdom: and with all thy getting get understanding.—Proverbs 4:7*

ACKNOWLEDGMENTS

Our sincere thanks to scientist Gustaf Stromberg and to Omar John Fareed, M.D., for their suggestions relative to those particular portions of this book touching on their fields of endeavor, which, however, in no way implies their endorsement of all the authors have said. Also especial gratitude is due Gertrude Dooley and Helen Carmack of *Science of Mind* magazine for their assistance in the preparation of the manuscript.

CONTENTS

INTRODUCTION

W HY ARE YOU interested in a new design for living? The odds are that in some aspect of your health, affairs, or relationships, things are not all that you desire them to be. In some way or other the pattern of your life and experience has not come up to your hopes and expectations. You feel a need to get out of your well-worn rut and move into a fuller, richer enjoyment of life. What can be done about establishing a new design for living in your personal experience? Two things:

First, there must be a willingness and desire to cut yourself loose from undesirable things of the past. This is not always easy, for all too often the way you have become accustomed to thinking along certain lines, and your tendency to accept as inevitable certain conditions and situations, have so ingrained themselves in your makeup—physically and mentally—that they are well-established habits. However, you can make the change and step out of what may have been an undesirable past into a bright new future.

Second, you will need to enlarge your viewpoint; develop an eagerness to encounter new ideas, evaluate them, and assimilate those which you can best use and adapt for your purposes and requirements. All too often a person finds that he has closed his mind to the very things which he desires most. Unconsciously there has developed a feeling that he knows all the answers and he is perfectly content to stand pat. The *status quo* becomes tolerable only because there is lack of initiative or enthusiasm to move onward, or sometimes because there is lack of knowledge as to what to do about it.

If you are willing, you can take these two steps leading to a new enjoyment of life.

No one can tell you what your new design for living should be, nor should anyone attempt to. This is for you to plan. You are your own architect, but some of the plans you have drawn in the past may have resulted in some structures of experience which have not been altogether good. You are not going to be supplied with a new set of blueprints. Rather, you are going to find out how to be a better architect. You are going to be provided with some new tools to work with, information about new building materials you can make use of, and better techniques of construction. With this new knowledge you can start with complete assurance that your new design for living will develop into a sound, strong, and more than satisfactory way of life that can include an abundance of all good things.

Nothing lies beyond the scope of your ability. The new design for living you create need have no limitations. Literally all the good things that life and the world offer are yours to have and enjoy. But you need to recognize them, accept them, and incorporate them into the new design you are now going to create.

Many will find that reading this book will be the start of their most important experience in living.

Naturally the question arises: What things are of the greatest importance to an individual? Inasmuch as you live in a world made up of your personal relationships to life, to conditions about you and your associations with others, one answer to the question would be: Whatever has the greatest bearing on constructive self-expression and helpfulness to others.

You want to live so as to get the most out of life, to have your unselfish personal ambitions fulfilled, and in so doing to contribute the most to others and to the age in which you live. In this connection you are going to learn how your thoughts or concepts affect you in regard to better health, greater happiness, and more success.

In doing this you will learn to develop a new outlook on life. While there are no deep or hidden secrets involved, there certainly are definite methods and techniques for scientifically as well as inspirationally discovering the answer to "What is it all about?" This does not mean that you are going to encounter dogmatic or opinionated ideas. It does mean that you will, after careful thought, decide for yourself what you believe about life, what you believe about your own destiny, what you believe about your relationship to others, and above all, what you believe about your relationship to that Power greater than you are which has created all things.

Everyone wishes to live creatively and expansively. So it is only natural that you should wish to uncover whatever undiscovered possibilities may be latent within you. Somehow or other everyone has a feeling that he is only half living, half expressing himself, and through some inward awareness, whether you call it intuition or not, you feel within you an echo of something deeper and bigger and broader and more expansive than that which you are now aware of. This feeling could not be there, could not be so universal, unless it had an element of reality behind it.

In all this you will be discovering how to cooperate better with the great mental, emotional, and spiritual laws of your being. It is most important to remember that you are not going to discover ideas whereby it will be easy-to-get-rich, easy-to-be-happy, easy-to-get-well; there are no such methods. But there are paths that may be followed which will lead to a richer, fuller experience of health and happiness, and a greater expression of the creative action of life.

There is a science of mind that can be used. It is not difficult to understand. It is simplicity itself, just as is everything that is wonderful and great. You will learn about this, and in learning you will find out for yourself the intimate relationship you have with a Principle within you that is greater than the intellect or will, and with a creative Power beyond all imagination.

Have joy in designing your new life. Try always to keep even the most profound things on the lighter side. Do not think everything has to be learned in a minute; do not become discouraged if all things are not accomplished in a day. Keep a good-natured flexibility, a happiness, and a spontaneous enthusiasm in what you are doing.

Once you undertake this new project it will not be too long before you can point to yourself and your experience and say with pride and satisfaction, "This is my life, and it is good."

A NEW
DESIGN
FOR LIVING

1 NEW THOUGHTS FOR OLD

We discover that the universe shows evidence of a designing or controlling power that has something in common with our own individual minds.

—SIR JAMES JEANS

As a BEGINNING let us take a long look, which should be a new look, at the world we live in. This can be our point of departure away from what has been and toward what we want things to be—the start of our new design for living.

In this connection, it might be wise to heed the advice of biochemist and Nobel Prize winner Dr. Albert Szent-Györgyi: "Research is to see what everybody has seen, and think what nobody has thought." It is often the meaning of the obvious in our everyday world which escapes us.

If a label were to be applied to the present-day world, it would be the Age of Science. An age of consistent logical thought; thought used to determine by experiment the nature of the physical world we live in. A ruthless endeavor to push forward the frontiers of discovery so that more of the Great Unknown, into which the physical seems to dissolve, becomes known.

Nothing is more certain than that things are not only what they appear to be, but are much, much more. Back of everything in life, back of everything in this world of ours, is the

3

unseen cause. Science attempts, in its endless research, to investigate the nature of this cause; to try to determine what it is, how it works, and, of the utmost importance, how to use it. Similarly, this is also the endeavor of unencumbered religion and philosophy, and should be the concern of every thinking man.

Just what do we mean when we say there is an unseen cause back of everything? The world encountered by the senses is very solid, very real, and very tangible. Appearances are one thing, but that which causes them are something else. At this point we encounter the laws or principles of nature which man has not seen and which in many respects he but dimly surmises. To illustrate this we need but look at any living thing— the seed you plant, a small animal, or more dramatically, the newborn babe. We see evidence of an organizing factor that assembles atoms into molecules, takes many different kinds of molecules and groups them together into cells of many varieties, and then assembles the cells so that a living thing, plant or animal, results. This is not a static bit of life, but a dynamic, growing, progressive life that exhibits an intelligent purpose!

Even within the atoms themselves there is a formative factor that makes the whole atomic world a thing of beauty, symmetry, and harmony. It takes the smallest subatomic particles and molds them into many different kinds of atoms; some with only one electron whirling about the complicated and still little-understood nucleus, and others with a hundred or more electrons surrounding it. It is out of these atoms, the basic building blocks of the universe, that the entire physical world we know is constructed—from the grain of sand to the rock, to the plant, to animal, man, and the farthest star. And these basic building blocks in their innermost action display the evidence of order, harmony, and intelligent organization.

Just as it is science's constant and sincere effort to discover the nature of the unseen cause back of all things, it should be our endeavor to discover within ourselves that determining factor which makes our life and experience what they are. In fact, properly approached, this could be the greatest of all sciences, and one in which the individual is both the laboratory and the experimenter.

Take a Look at Yourself

Our own mind and thought are the only things we have to work with. Without them, without intelligence or the ability to think, we would be unable to do anything, we would have no conscious existence. To find out how our mind works through the process of thought is really to discover what enables "the brain to think, the feet to walk, and the ears to hear."

Actually we seek to discover our real self, that which is back of what we appear to be. Of necessity there must be something, however intangible it may seem, which stands back of our actions and commands them. We know ourselves to a large degree as we appear in the physical world, but we need to come to understand the *real* self—the unseen cause that brought us forth.

When we look at ourselves carefully we find that we possess a physical body that has certain dimensions and occupies a definite amount of space; then we discover the fact that back of this there is a nondimensional mind, something which we don't see. So we are led to believe that just as the physical body is composed of the same basic elements of which all things with physical form are made, elements which show signs of order, harmony, and an intelligent organization at work, so it must be that our minds are also rooted in some larger unseen realm. It would also follow that since man is whole, a unity of mind and body, we must look beyond appearances to that fundamental Something, which we may call Spirit, which is the immediate source of both, that Something which is *both* mind and body.

We want to discover and demonstrate for ourselves that there is within us, invisible but real, that which is the dominating creative factor of our minds and bodies and which also extends its creativity into our experience. Once we begin this search we will never be satisfied until we have proved our discovery by creating a new world of experience for ourselves.

In order to do this it will be necessary to follow the pathway of all scientific investigation. Our minds must be cleared of all limiting ideas. We begin with a child's sense of discovery which enables us to be ready to accept the new and marvelous world we will encounter Once we are able to do this we will realize that there is a Power greater than we are, even though we use It, and know that there is an Intelligence, beyond our conscious knowledge, which flows through us.

We are living in a universe of order, not one of chaos. Just as there are principles and laws in the physical world which we must become aware of and ascertain the proper methods and techniques of using, so there are spiritual and mental laws which we must likewise come to know and use. In both instances we accept the principles involved and make use of the proved techniques.

Keep in mind the fact that principles are not tangible as far as the five senses are concerned; but this in no way affects their validity, any more than we would think gravity does not exist because we cannot neatly do it up in a package. In much the same manner love, beauty, and harmony are very definite realities that are also intangible but wield a tremendous force in this world of ours. The mere fact that we cannot weigh or measure a principle or law in no way detracts from its effectiveness. The entire physical world which we encounter in our daily experience emanates from an unseen world. ". . . things which are seen were not made of things which do appear."

Discover New Worlds

"Thoughts are things." Matter is mind in form, mind is matter unformed. Very interesting if true, and if true the implications are tremendous. What foundation can we discover that could lead us to believe such a conclusion is valid and logical? Let us take a more considered look at the world about us and try to ascertain its relationship to the unseen world of the mind.

Very few of us have had the opportunity or the inclination to work in any of the many fields of science. But that is no reason why the results of the work that is being done should not be of interest to us. In fact, many of the stories and photographs appearing in newspapers and magazines could have a greater significance for us if we would read and look at them with a fresh viewpoint.

Orderly Atoms

Have you ever seen X-ray diffraction photographs? They are photographs showing the inner structure of crystals or metals as revealed by the paths of X-rays through them. What do they look like? The pictures have pinpoints of light arranged in regular and symmetrical patterns, sometimes circular, other times linear. The X-rays have bounced off the atoms or molecules comprising the substance under examination, indicating their orderly and regular arrangement.

The most precise and accurate clock that man has yet been able to devise, one which is the master timepiece for the country, is not controlled by springs or weights, or even by the more reliable method of using the vibrations of a quartz crystal. The heart of the clock, the basis of its phenomenal accuracy, is the ammonia molecule. When certain atoms or molecules are excited by a sufficient amount of energy they start to vibrate. Nothing now known to man is more constant than this rate of vibration. And from these vibrating atoms or molecules, through a sequence of electronic components, a frequency-controlled flow of power is derived which moves the hands of a clock. How accurate is it? Previously man has used the sun, the planets, and the stars to regulate the accuracy of a master timepiece, but those astronomical bodies now seem to be far less accurate than they were supposed to be. A vibrating molecule has a constancy which seems impossible to surpass, and a molecular clock does not vary more than one second in three hundred years! And this variation no doubt resides in the parts of the clock, not in the molecule.

Everyday Wonders

Salt and sugar are very common in our everyday life, but have you ever looked at such crystals under a microscope, or seen pictures of them? They are wonders of symmetry. Minerals and gems, yes, even the diamond, also show such crystalline structure. Do you remember ever eating rock candy? Have you ever made some by hanging a string in a jar in which a quantity of sugar has been dissolved? It is fascinating to see the crystals start to grow on the string and get larger and larger, building up layer after layer until they get quite large.

Snow is a wonderful sight, but there is more beauty to a snowflake than you probably have yet realized. Catch a large flake on the sleeve of your coat and examine it with a magnifying glass, being careful not to breathe on it, for it melts easily. It is a thing of unparalleled beauty, but remember you are looking at only one snowflake, and there are never two alike. Crystals again. Crystals that began as drops of moisture high in the sky. Some are very simple, others very complicated and ornate. Some snowflakes are even double-deckers. Regardless of their size, regardless of the degree of ornateness in the design, the basic design is always the same: the snowflake is fundamentally a six-pointed star.

Have you ever seen a cross section of the trunk of a giant sequoia tree, or a picture of it? Ring after ring of growth. One ring for each year, and there are thousands of them, each year's growth of cells neatly circling the previous year's growth. You can find the same thing in a branch of the tree in your own back yard. Pick a leaf from that tree. Look at the regular tracery of veins which supply the leaf with water and minerals.

It is magnificent. And take a look at the bush beneath the tree. Is there a spider web in it? It is neatly woven in a lacy design. And strong—stronger than structural steel. Some of the threads are sticky to entrap insects, others are slick providing pathways for the spider. Perhaps you have stirred up a grasshopper who bounded off with one long jump. He can jump a long way. But think about that jump. Proportionately, the most powerful jump among all living things. A terrific amount of power and a use of leverage that is fantastic.

No doubt many times you have gathered pretty shells on the beach or along a stream bed. Very pretty shells. But did you examine them? Masterpieces of engineering; internal patterns of curvature and progressive growth that require complicated mathematics to describe. A structure of rigidity and strength far surpassing man's engineering skills.

Do you like honey? Honey that you get in a comb? Tastes good. But did you ever really take a good look at a honeycomb? All the cells are hexagonal, the perfect shape for strength and conservation of space.

You have all seen pictures of the human skeleton, or seen an actual skeleton in a museum. Perhaps you were not the least bit interested. Next time look more carefully. Superb! Perfect adaptation of structure to purpose. Light in weight, nothing superfluous. Mobility of joints. The bones themselves? Hard-cased on the outside, with an elaborate harmonious network of delicate but strong supporting bony material inside.

Perhaps you have at some time had an electrocardiogram taken. On the strip of paper that passes through the recording machine are traced wavy lines indicating the rhythmic beat of your heart. On a long recording the tracery is a beautiful repetitive pattern with all the peaks and valleys harmoniously spaced and appearing at regular intervals. Feel your pulse, it is consistent and harmonious. How many times do you breathe a minute? Watch someone else breathe; notice the regularity of the rise and fall of the chest.

A New Outlook

What is it that we are trying to discover? Are we trying to find what we might have previously overlooked in ordinary everyday things? It would appear that there is much more to learn than meets the eye, although the eye can give us clues and hints about the thing we are seeking.

Why did that drop of water which became a snowflake develop into a six-pointed structure? Before the drop became a snowflake, something determined the basic shape that would develop. Something determined that the two atoms of hydrogen and one of oxygen, which comprise water, would, when in a suitable atmospheric situation, become a flake with a definite crystalline structure.

Water crystallized as snowflake or ice, or any crystal in nature, provides the physicist with nothing but atoms from which it was built. But when certain atoms are brought together in a regular and orderly manner, a crystal with a definite geometrical form must result. We know that a fertile chicken egg will produce a baby chick. We know that two tiny cells, comprised of atoms which are joined together within it, will grow into thousands of cells, and in the process of growing some will become bone, others flesh, others feathers. What is that something back of both the crystal and the chick that takes the atoms and arranges them, joins them together, adding more and more, and finally assembles them into the end result?

Does that something reside within the atom itself? In this concretion of pure energy, comprised of a nucleus surrounded by orbiting electrons, is it here that all the intelligence, purpose, and essence of form that are found in the physical world reside? We don't know. But it does not seem logical or possible. Even if the atom does contain within itself the source and the pattern of all physical things, how did such a power get in the atom? Rather, it would appear, the physical world did not develop of its own accord, or out of the action of electrical charges, but instead there is an organizing factor that uses the atoms to construct things.

What would have to be the nature of it?

First Things First

The astronomer says that the planets and the stars in the heavens evidence an arrangement and behavior that signifies that there is an intelligence behind what we ascertain, an intelligence that is infinite and that is mathematical in its thought. And that regardless of where man looks in the skies he will always discover that the stars are built of the same kind of atoms which we find here on earth.

The physicist says that the mathematical relationships of the elements of matter are real and not imaginary, and that mathematics is a concept of thought, based on laws of logical thinking; that the concept or idea of any mathematical orderliness in the physical world must of necessity precede the appearance of such orderliness.

The biologist finds living things, things comprised of atoms, exhibiting a purpose and a goal. Atoms, the building blocks of the universe, do not build of their own accord. Something has to do the building.

The theoretical physicist says that energy and mass are interchangeable, that matter is congealed energy. The practical physicist has demonstrated this. Pure energy may take form as a material particle; and the particle in turn may become pure energy. The invisible becoming visible, the visible becoming invisible. In explaining the nature of the physical world Nobel Prize winner physicist Werner Heisenberg stated, ". . . there is only one fundamental substance of which all reality consists. If we have to give this substance a name, we can only call it 'energy.' But this fundamental 'energy' is capable of existence in different forms." Zoologist C. Lloyd Morgan observed that "If we acknowledge a physical basis of so-called matter and energy as ultimately involved in all natural events, may we not also acknowledge God as the directive activity on Whom the manner of going in all natural events ultimately depends?"

The Greatest of All Forces

It would appear that the greatest of all forces, the power, the infinite directive factor in and back of the universe is something that we are forced to label Mind or Intelligence. Mind or Intelligence which is orderly and harmonious as evidenced in the results of Its action. This action we describe and define in terms of law, but our definition of such laws will always be subject to refinement, and as we become more aware of the real nature of the action we are investigating there will be a deeper understanding.

Mind also appears to be the ultimate source of energy, and energy is Mind in action. Energy is the essence of atoms. Atoms are the building blocks of every physical thing. That which creates is the same as the thing created. The cause is the same as the effect. Thoughts are things. And all is in perfect accord with law, all a function of Mind or Intelligence.

What we term our mind cannot be other than part of the universal Mind; there is nothing else for it to be part of. The One Mind is always creative, directive; the cause back of everything. Our minds, being part of It, would have to be creative to a certain degree. Raynor C. Johnson, physicist, in this connection has said, "The outside world of objects may thus be regarded as originating in a sustained field created by the Divine Mind—with which our minds are in a kind of rapport." It is logical to assume that the degree of our creativity is determined by our awareness and use of the laws by which it operates. What we don't know about we can't use or direct.

Unrealized Potentialities

When we have come to accept the idea that there is an unseen yet ultimate Reality back of us and our world, that this

Reality is intelligent and conscious, that our own mind or consciousness emanates from It, and as a result must partake of Its nature, then we see that limitless unrealized potentialities lie before us. But these potentialities must of necessity conform to principles and laws. And whenever principles and laws are encountered, there are proper methods and techniques for their use.

From the ideas which have been advanced so far, some might say that all we have been doing is talking about God. Perhaps so. But God means different things to different people. Too many people have too limited a concept of God. As we enlarge our thinking, we can enlarge our concept of God. So in order not to have our thinking limited by what we may have previously thought, or influenced by what others may say or think, we start out with a new set of ideas and concepts which are unfettered and free to grow and develop.

With this in mind we can say that there is One Reality, Mind, or Intelligence back of all things—a spiritual Source, an Infinite. Call It God if you desire. But be sure that the term by which you call It is in no way limited by your previous way of thinking.

There are many ways to approach this Reality, Life Itself. Learning more about the world we live in is just another way of learning more about the unseen or spiritual cause of our life and the way it works. It is possible that some of the ideas you may encounter here are not wholly acceptable or understandable at the time. If so, do not argue with them, set them aside on a mental shelf for a while. Later on come back to them; then their full importance may be realized. In any event, do not throw the wheat out with what might now be considered chaff, for we do not want any immediate disagreement with the ideas presented to prevent the acceptance of a later idea which could be the "pearl of great price."

The world we live in is all that it appears to be, but it is also much more.

There is the unseen cause—the intelligence or purpose in and through all things.

Ephemeral and intangible as it may seem, this cause, which can only be described as a form of thought, is the basic Reality of the universe.

Such thought is the action or function of a supreme consciousness which may be defined as Mind, Spirit, or God.

2
ADVENTURES IN THINKING

Human thought is an integral part of the universe, of the cosmos . . .

—LECOMTE DU NOÜY

ONE OF THE GREATEST DISCOVERIES man has ever made, or ever can make, is the discovery of the creative power of his thought. But with this discovery there must come the realization that our thinking is creative not because we will or wish or hope or long that it may be so, but because it is a principle of nature that it be so.

This could only mean, when we stop to think about it, that we do not put creativity into our thinking, but take it out. This is true of every force in nature. Power is intrinsically there, we only use and direct it.

One of the fundamental steps we need to take in creating a new design for living is the recognition that we are dealing with a Power that makes things out of Itself by Itself becoming the thing that It makes. There is no separation between Creator and creation, they are one and the same thing. They are different sides of the same coin. When we think about it, is not this the way everything is created? Is not everything made out of that which cannot be seen? Is not the invisible always becoming visible in accord with a form or pattern? What about that rosebush in the garden? There must be some thought, plan, or pattern for its structure which defies man's engineering skill, and even his ability to comprehend fully the way it operates. In what mind did that idea originate? Not ours. It had to be a Mind greater than ours—that Mind which also expresses as our minds, and of which our minds are a part.

Whenever we reach the point where we realize that our thought is creative not because of our wish or will, but because this is its nature, then we can see how it might be possible to help ourselves through the process of properly directed thought. We will then know that in helping ourselves we are not using some mysterious power of concentration, some unknown force, but rather are consciously using the creative energy of the mind, which, once recognized, may be definitely and specifically employed.

Your Mind and Brain

So far we have just been talking about the mind. No doubt many are inquiring about the brain. What happened to it? Where does it fit into the picture? Many people, including some men of science, feel that the brain is all there is, that there is nothing beyond it. From this viewpoint they are entirely justified in their conclusions that man, all that he is, all that he creates, all that he feels, all that he senses of beauty, of value, of right, and all that he strives to achieve are only the results of the mechanical relationships of billions of cells in the brain and the attendant flow of electrical charges or chemical actions from one cell to another.

There is no question but that the brain is a tremendous mechanism. The electronic brains and calculating machines man has built are also wonders, and they are being made bigger and better all the time. But it is beyond man's wildest dream that he will ever be able to duplicate the operation of the brain of man. Even if he were to do so, could he ever create consciousness?

There is no indication that the brain of man itself, or the electronic brain man has built, will ever be able to produce the words of a Shakespeare, create on canvas a Sistine Madonna, or convey the love that passes from a mother to the child at her breast. To say this could happen would be just as senseless as saying that the dictionary is the result of an explosion in a type foundry!

The only logical conclusion which can be reached is that there must be Something beyond the physical brain. About this, for the most part, men of medicine remain silent. Not necessarily because they do not recognize that there must be something beyond the brain, but rather perhaps because they probably feel that the subject lies beyond the scope of their professional activity. However, more and more of them are becoming outspoken. Dr. Irvine H. Page, director of research at the famed Cleveland Clinic, has said in effect that although the brain may be likened to a computer, a series of complex electrical circuits, a *mind* is required to control the brain, and unidentified forces are expressed through the brain as thought.

The brain, it is true, is a physical mechanism, but there must be an operator. An engine is of no value without an engineer. An electronic brain is useless unless there is a mind to direct its activity. Behind every activity there must be an actor. Things do not happen unless there is something to make them happen. The brain is a machine, but behind it there must be a thinker to make it operate—a mind. And such a mind can only have its being and source in the one infinite Mind. Without the direction of the mind, the brain would be but a useless mass of tissue. The coordinating and directing factor must always be superior, over and above that which is coordinated and directed. By the same token, man's individual mind, being a part of the infinite Mind, will always be subordinate to It; the lesser can ever encompass more of the larger, but never include all of It.

What Is Mind?

We may feel that our minds are *our* minds. That they are individual entities having no connection or relationship with anything else. It is important that we change our thinking in this respect. World-famed physiologist Sir Charles Sherrington once wrote: ". . . perceiving mind and the perceived world . . . are both parts of one mind. . . ." No one has ever shown the least ability to create mind. Nor could any happenstance in nature ever evolve it. Certainly the brain is a thing that has resulted from the action of biological law in the development of the human body, but as we have just seen, that is not enough. There is the mind, that immeasurable, intangible thing which did not come out of the nowhere and nothing. It has to have a source and that source could only be something like it, the One Mind or Intelligence.

Well-known physicist Paul E. Sabine found himself forced to the conclusion that it becomes necessary to "identify the rational element of the human mind with the rational element of the Universe and the creative power of human thought with the creative energy which is the physical world."

In reality, when we use our minds, when we think, we are thinking *with* and *in* the One Mind and It is always reacting to us, and Its reaction is in accord with the way we think. When we consider our thought in this way and the possibilities implied, we find that the potential of our thought is beyond our highest imagination and our greatest dream of good.

Regardless of what our feeling about it may be at this time, the creative process of our thought is very simple. In fact, so simple that it likely escapes our understanding. We overlook the obvious and seek to confuse, complicate, and become terribly involved about something that is very simple, simple to the point that it confounds us.

What is it that is so simple, plain, and obvious? Nothing more than this: It is done unto us as we believe! When we consider this idea in connection with thought in the form of prayer, we must believe we have what we have prayed for, then we *will* have it. In this way prayer becomes its own answer through the creative nature of thought, whether it be used for the healing of illness or the betterment of conditions. And what is effective prayer other than the process of thought being clearly directed for a greater experience of good for ourselves or others?

Your Freedom to Think

How are we directing our thought? We are free to think in any direction we choose. There is nothing that says we have to think one way or another. Just as there could be no restrictions on the thought of God, so there are no restrictions on what we think. We alone may determine what thoughts we desire to entertain. This prerogative on our part seems to get us into trouble, probably, more easily than it gets us out of trouble. Why? For one reason or another we find ourselves surrounded by people who are wallowing in fear. Fear of this and that, fear of anything that comes along. We seem to be afraid of anything we do not know about. We fear what an ache may mean, we fear what tomorrow will bring, we fear we may lose what we have. If and when a fear becomes something specific we know what we have to cope with and can do something about it. But until then we seem to be fearful of everything. Fear is nothing but a process of thought and thought is creative. So we come to experience what we have feared! Logical. Sad but true. But, once we are aware of what our patterns of thinking may have done to create the undesirable situation we find ourselves in today, we are in a position to switch from creating what we don't desire to building a future which will contain the abundance, harmony, and perfection that has to reside at the heart of the universe. We got ourselves into the trouble we may now find ourselves in, and we can just as easily get ourselves out of it.

We began by saying that the greatest discovery man could ever make was the discovery of the creative power of his own thought. Perhaps the greatest achievement man can attain to is the creative use of his thought for the experiencing of greater good in every aspect of living.

Plus and Minus Thinking

It would probably be correct to say that *every* thought we have is in some way and to some degree creative. What we need to do is to add them up, plus and minus, and see what kind of total we get. Do we think one thought of health during the day and the rest of the time concentrate on our aches and pains? Do we toss off a quick prayer at night in the hope that it will compensate for all we may have done wrong during the day? We need to consider our thought as a pair of scales, one side good, the other side bad. Through our thinking which side are we adding to? The side with the greatest weight is that which we have selected to experience.

In this respect, inasmuch as every thought is creative, every thought may be considered as a form of prayer. From this point of view, what is the nature of our prayers? Do they affirm or deny the good we desire? Prayer is only a form of thought, and negative prayers can create negative experiences! This has been dramatically proved by the research work of Professor William R. Parker of Redlands University. In his investigation into prayer therapy he has discovered that "unless prayer is positive it may be dangerous. The thoughts or desires we hold eventually conquer and control our lives."

In considering our world of the mind, its nature, and how it works, we find ourselves faced with the necessity of being ever on our guard as to what we permit ourselves to think. This does not mean that we limit our thinking or bar ourselves from growth and new ideas. We have to continually expand our ability to think and encounter new ideas. But we do not have to entertain those ideas which are negative, which deprive us of happiness, create ill-health, or limit our bank account. We cannot help thinking, but we can learn to think in a way that is for our betterment rather than our detriment. Not only can we learn to think in this way, it is our obligation to ourselves, to others, and to our Maker to do so. We have no right, deliberately or unconsciously, to deprive the Life within us of the fullest possible expression or bar ourselves from the abundance of all good things which are ours for the accepting.

So we find ourselves confronted with the most fascinating and dramatic possibilities that life can offer. We have conscious access to a creative Power which is ready, willing, and able to respond to us constructively, but which we may be using only to our detriment. Our conscious and specific use of It is limited to our awareness or understanding of It. This is not a unique thing but applies to every law in nature. And when any law is used for the securing of certain results it must be used in a specific and right manner. Spiritual and mental laws must be thought of in the same manner as any physical law. When we learn to do this we will find that a new design for living will be created in our experience in a logical manner.

Your Partnership with the Infinite

Famous physicist and Nobel Prize winner Robert A. Millikan said in effect that the Architect of the universe had brought man this far in his physical development and provided him with a mind, but now it was up to man to use his mind, to let that great Intelligence and Creativity operate and flow through him; man has reached the point where he is a co-creator in his world.

In our world of experience we are co-creators with the Architect of the universe! Are we doing a good job? Or are we making a mess of things, inhibiting the natural harmony and order that exist at the center of everything? Are we depriving ourselves of the natural growth, purpose, and expression of the supreme Mind in and through us, trying to live according to the dictates of what we ourselves have dreamed up? Most people have dreamed up some pretty horrible things which they are now experiencing.

Everything that is visible, everything that we experience, is but an effect of something that occurs in the invisible, something that occurs in the infinite Mind, or through our use of that Mind. In the intangible realm of the spiritual world, in the Mind of God, a pattern for everything we see originates and exists. From the individual atom to man himself there is one continuous unbroken chain of progression reflecting intelligent purpose and design. A basic pattern does exist, although there are infinite expressions of it and a progressive growth exhibiting a striving and a purpose toward an ultimate goal which we may yet but dimly see. This pattern of thought in Mind would have to be perfect at all times or else there could never be a semblance of that perfection in nature which we discover exists with mathematical beauty and elegance.

When in our experience things sometimes seem good and at other times bad, we need only examine our ideas to determine the cause. Cause there must be, and that cause has to reside in our thought, for it is only through thought that things become tangible and are sustained. An experience can be resolved to a cause that is a thought continuing to maintain and sustain itself according to law, and expressing itself according to the idea it contains. If things are not what they should be, we change our thought, change the patterns or ideas which control our experiences.

The least we can do is to create mental patterns of what we want rather than what we don't want. We did not create the physical universe, but we can and do decide what our relationship to it will be. We did not create our bodies, but, as psychosomatic medicine has now discovered, what we do to our mind-body relationship determines the degree of health we may experience. And what we may have miscreated in the past can be changed. Change the thought or pattern and the form or experience will change.

Mental Merry-go-rounds

Mind and matter, pattern and tangible form, thought and experience—in every instance the first determines the second. One is the cause, the other the effect. When we pattern our thinking according to experiences of failure, unhappiness, or ill-health, what are we doing to ourselves? We are letting a negative idea become the cause of more negative experiences and we find ourselves caught in a vicious circle. This circular chain of events will continue to repeat itself with monotonous regularity. We need to step in consciously, break the sequence and start thinking anew in accord with the results we desire. Otherwise ill-health could maintain itself, as could poverty. Perhaps to a certain extent we are all on such a merry-go-round in one manner or another. But once we discover that we have the right and the ability to initiate a new sequence, to use the creative power of our own minds in a better way, then we can step off our dizzy ride, regain our equilibrium, and start going in a straight path toward our desired goal.

All of this is not a deep mystery, way over our heads, or too difficult to understand. We may just accept it all, as we do other things in life, and come to the simple conclusion that our mental, emotional, and spiritual reactions to life underlie and influence everything that happens to us. That is all there is to it. But the concept is so great, so fraught with potentialities, that we have not yet even begun to scratch the surface of what it can mean to us.

Start a New Habit

The practice of right thinking for the purpose of producing definite desired results is of utmost simplicity. It simmers down to the essential fact that we should make a habit of entertaining in mind only those thoughts and ideas which we wish to experience in outward form. If the experience is not right, change the thought or pattern which is the cause of it. We should so change our pattern of thinking that it more nearly expresses and coincides with that perfection which resides in Mind–God. God by definition is perfect, and examination of His handiwork reveals this perfection. Let us avail ourselves of it. As we do, automatically a better condition or situation will result; back of everything there is one great and good Cause that can and will flow into and through everything in our experience.

A new design for living needs to have a source, a pattern, before it can ever appear in our lives. The architect needs to have an idea before he can start using his pencil. The idea is first. Illustrative of this, and of our relationship to the creativity inherent in the Universe, is this statement by Plotinus, the famous third-century philosopher whose work climaxed seven hundred years of creative thinking: "Thought and thing depend upon and correspond to each other. What is real is not the aggregation of ponderable matter, but the laws which the Soul makes and finds there. Each individual soul is a little 'first cause' . . . we understand Nature best by looking above what is merely presented to our senses. What is free in us is that spontaneous movement of the Spirit which has no external cause."

If we can become aware that, right now, we are living in a universe that is spiritual, with pure Consciousness at its center, and that such a universe would have to be governed by this Intelligence acting as Law; and if we can realize that we are individualized points of consciousness in this One Power, then we can see that each one has an intimate and personal relationship with both the infinite Presence which flows through all things and the universal Law through which all things are manifest.

This is a basic idea which we are going to use. It means that each of us may control his experience to a degree beyond all present expectations, and do so entirely in accord with law in the spiritual world. For it is the action of thought in the spiritual or mental world which governs our experience in the physical world, whether it be our bodies or our affairs.

Nothing Is Static

The question might be raised that a certain physical condition has been created and that is that. There it is, tangible and real. That is the end of the road and nothing more can be done. Or that a certain situation has been established in our affairs and appears to be unchangeable. When such ideas come to mind we need to remember that nothing is static. At no point or level of activity in the physical world or in our world of experience are things ever at a standstill. All is action. All is energy. All moves in accord with law. Nothing is changeless. The only thing constant is change, the necessary expression of a creativity which flows from the Mind of the Universe, which is ceaseless in Its action. Regardless of appearances there is always a continuing creative action behind them. There is always a pattern of thought, a spiritual or mental mold, behind everything.

In big construction projects we see small board after small board being properly placed together. Soon they create a massive form into which concrete is poured. What form does the concrete take? It has no choice other than to conform with the mold which has been prepared. There is no limit to the size or the shape of the mold which may be created. So it is with our thoughts. One by one we entertain them in our consciousness. They establish the total mold or pattern of our entire body of thought, which in turn becomes the form for our experience.

For this reason doctors are often at a loss in assisting a sick person to get well. They may be able to correct one specific condition only to discover that within a very short time the patient is back again with another serious ailment. It would appear that the patient has a pattern of thought that spells "sickness." If the doctor removes a possibility of sickness in one direction, then the tendency to be sick will appear in another and entirely unrelated place.

It is always good objectively to do all we can to cope with any effect, physically or in our affairs, but the real and final solution to any problem can only be found by working at the level of prime causation, that of thought—the spiritual level. If we stick a needle in the end of our finger there is considerable pain. Certainly the pain can be alleviated by the use of an anesthetic, but once it wears off the pain is back again. To remove the cause of the pain we have to remove the needle. In much the same manner we remove or change patterns of thinking which create undesirable experiences.

Do You Know What You Are Doing?

In coming into a realization that we may consciously better ourselves through right thinking, we must at the same time know that the reason for our being able to do so is the fact that we are using a Power greater than we are. It is only through our understanding of Its nature that we are able to use It in a definite and right manner for specific purposes. The desired results will not be brought about in a minute, although theoretically it should be possible. Rather we seem to have to build up or change our thought patterns gradually. We achieve a little here and then a little there, until finally the main body of our thought is affirmative and constructive.

Until the time a person becomes aware of the creative nature of his thought, he has been creating his destiny without knowing it, not even suspecting that such a process has been taking place. The tragedy and unhappiness brought on by the unknowing and unconscious misdirection of this creative process of thought is appalling as we look about us, or even examine our own lives.

Henry Van Dyke wrote·

We build our future, thought by thought,
For good or ill, yet know it not.

But now we seek to change all this. We endeavor consciously, definitely, and deliberately to determine what we will experience through the conscious decision to place in our minds only those thoughts which we desire to have reproduced in our experience. Again and again we need to remind ourselves, first of the nature, extent, and power of the invisible Principle we are using, and next of the simplicity of using It.

Reliable Law

We need never explain why thought is creative, or what life is, or why law exists. No one can ever do this. But we can discover for ourselves, and demonstrate in our own lives, that there is a Principle of Mind, that It does work, that we can use It, and that It will never fail us.

The fact that It never fails us is both to our advantage and disadvantage. It always works. Not just occasionally, not sometimes, but all the time. The fact that our thought is creative at all means that it is creative all the time, and that creative action is governed by law which never ceases to be. Regardless of where a person might be, the color of his skin, the clothes he wears, the religious customs he observes, as long as he thinks, as long as there is a process of thought in his mind, then that thought does have a creativity inherent in it. This creativity is mandatory; we have no choice as to whether our thought will be creative or not, it just is. But we do have a choice as to the content of our thought which is the causative creative factor in our experience.

We find that we must of necessity choose very carefully every element of our new design for living. We have to be sure that the broad general idea of the new structure of experience we desire to build is sound and desirable. Then, as we select specific ideas to be used in filling in the details of the basic concept, we must be alert that no element creeps in that could ever endanger the project. That there is no drop of ink to discolor the glass of water. Simple. Easy to do. But it necessitates vigilance.

Thought can be creative of our good and it can also be productive of things we do not desire, for all thought is creative.

Whether our thought patterns be for our benefit or detriment makes no difference to the Law of Mind; Its law acts impersonally.

Any problem or difficulty must lie within our use of our mind, in our misdirected thinking, not in the action of the Law, nor in the nature of Mind–God, which can only be good.

3

DON'T LIMIT YOURSELF

*. . . that I—I in the widest meaning of the
word, that is to say, every conscious mind that
has ever said or felt "I"—am the person, if
any, who controls the "motions of the atoms"
according to the laws of nature.*

—ERWIN SCHRÖDINGER

IF IT IS TRUE that *it is done unto us as we believe* it becomes
apparent that there must be Something that *does* something
according to our belief, but that this Something is limited in
Its doing according to the way we think. Hence we are confronted with the necessity of enlarging our concepts and of
thinking clearly. We have found that there is an ultimate yet
unseen Reality or Cause back of all things. We also have discovered that our own mind or consciousness is part of the infinite Mind, and as a result partakes of Its nature. A sign of
the times is that in all fields of scientific inquiry it is becoming
more and more evident that the creative power of our minds
stems from the creative nature of the Universe Itself!

Mathematician A. Cressy Morrison wrote: "Progress has now
been sufficient for us to see that God seems to be giving man
a spark of His own Intelligence." Once we step into the laboratory of our own minds we will discover this for ourselves,
and realize that our thought is creative in all aspects of our

experience. What we need to do is to learn to use it specifically for the good we desire. The use of it for the creation of good in our experience has been designated by many different names—creative affirmative prayer, meditation, spiritual mind treatment, positive thinking. It doesn't matter what you care to call it, the fact is established that a certain directed process of thought, an intangible and unseen thing, does have an effect on our experience and on our relationship to the world in which we live.

Remove Superstitions

We have come to realize that Mind in Action is a creative Law which is everywhere and at all times operative. It is a neutral and impersonal force as far as we are concerned. This applies to all law, regardless of its nature, otherwise it would not be universal and hence would not be law.

This may raise the question of whether the impersonal operation of the Law of Mind implies that there is something opposed to God, to infinite Intelligence. Whether there is God and a devil, whether there is good and bad in the Universe, or whether there are two final powers forever in opposition to each other. But such is not the case. Rightly considered, conclusions of this type are based on superstition and figments of the imagination, not on the evidence we may discover within our own minds or in the world about us.

Consider the nature of the soil of the earth, the medium in which seeds rest and find the sustenance for their growth and development. There is no withholding on the part of the soil of anything in it which the seed needs. The soil is impartial, giving alike to all seeds. Be it flower or weed, the soil supplies to each its need according to the demands that are made upon it. If we plant weeds in our garden, weeds will grow. It does no good to plant weeds and wish they were flowers. But we can choose to plant flowers and uproot any weeds that may have drifted in. In the same way we can plant in our minds desirable thoughts and learn to discard those thoughts which are undesirable.

The Law of Mind always acts, and the result of that action is always in perfect accord with the nature of the thought that was the motivation. However, it must not be overlooked that back of the reaction of the Law to our thought there is that Divine and infinite Intelligence which will guide us rightly in our choice of thought if we recognize and let It.

Things Can Change

We need have no concern over the fact that the Law of Mind in Action, when motivated, may produce sickness or health, poverty or abundance, happiness or unhappiness. These things It cannot do of Its own accord. The thought has to come first. Whether we like it or not, this is the way things are, this is the way the Law of Mind works. But we should rejoice in this knowledge for it means that things can change, that no law of its own accord deliberately imposes unwanted situations and conditions on us. We do not have to resign ourselves to a fate not to our liking. Nothing prescribes that we endure trial and tribulation except our own thinking!

If this were not the case we would be only automatons, robots, senseless mechanical organisms. We are individuals; we do have a mind; we do think; we do have consciousness. We do have the power of choice, to choose to exercise the creative power of our thought for our good—a choice and a power that is inherent within us.

The Way Law Works

No law ever takes the initiative. It can't. It isn't the nature of any law to do so. A law describes an action, within our ability adequately to describe the action. In dealing with the physical world, when scientists have proved time and time again that certain things result when certain other things are done, they define the action that occurs in terms of law. A law explains how cause leads to effect. Actually there is no difference between cause and effect, one just precedes the other. Similarly we say there is no difference between thought and thing, but the way of one becoming the other is defined as law. And the relationship that exists between one state and the other, and the process of that relationship being established, is always the same, never varying. It is law—the way things work—not a causative factor in and of itself.

For this reason we cannot say of the things which do appear in our experience that some were the result of the operation of a force of evil in our lives, or that others were the result of some particular benevolent activity in our favor. If there is law in the universe at all, if there is one creative Power back of all things, a Power that could not be divided against Itself, then we find that what may occur to us in any way is but the result of our use of that Power. Have we used It wisely? But regardless of the fact that we may have previously used It unwisely, we are in no way obligated to continue to do so. We think all the time. We can change the pattern of our thinking, and the response of the Law to the new pattern of thought will be just as sure as it was to the old, only a new effect that corresponds to the new thought will result. Maurice Maeterlinck concisely expressed this idea when he wrote: "Nothing befalls us that is not of the nature of ourselves. There comes no adventure but wears to our soul the shape of our everyday thoughts."

When we come to understand the way in which thought produces our experience, we awake to the fact that we should be exceedingly careful that nothing enters or is retained in our consciousness except that which is good. This must always be our final criterion. We need no other, nor need we be concerned with any other person's opinion about it. If our whole desire is to do good, to be helpful, to live constructively, then there is no reason at all why we should not expect to encounter good in every phase of our own personal experience. When we come to think and act in this way and enjoy the benefits which will ensue, those benefits will in no way deprive another of anything; rather, the good which results from the creative action of our own right thought will not only enhance our experience but that of those about us.

We need continually to remind ourselves that there are not two final powers in the Universe. There is but One, and It is good. Those things which appear to be destructive, or the opposite of good, have no final reality in Mind or God which would make our experience of them mandatory. Rather we would seem to be temporarily reaping the undesired results of our wrong and negative use of ideas!

The Cornerstone of Freedom

In considering the new design for living we desire to create, we find that it is in our own mind that we have the ways and means to build, and build well. Not only do we find that in the process of thinking we have the ability to think in any manner that we choose without any limitation, but also that there is no restriction on the creativity which is inherent in thought. We have here both the raw material of which our experience is created and the means by which it is created. The process by which the raw material, the content of thought, becomes experience is automatic, the operation of Law. We don't have to make one become the other, it just does.

Of prime importance is what kind of raw materials we are going to use. What are we going to think? We discover that we have to lift ourselves out of the mental ruts we have been traveling in to discover new raw materials. Bigger, better ideas are needed, ideas free from the limitations imposed by our past thinking which certainly in many respects has been far from adequate in designing a completely satisfactory way of life.

And as we proceed to do this we always need to keep firmly in mind, and never deviate from, the basis for our endeavor. This basis is: There is one Mind, Intelligence, Spirit, or God, which is the source of all that exists and this source is good. Our own ignorance and lack of understanding are the only sources of our undesirable conditions and situations, and the only things that need to be overcome. And it is through increasing wisdom, knowledge, and understanding that we may grow out of our ignorance and achieve a fuller life. It is often said that ignorance is the only sin, and enlightenment the only salvation. And in such degree as we cooperate with and entertain good in our thought and actions, the entire nature of the Universe is for us and nothing is against us. In such degree as we consciously or unconsciously associate our thought with other than good we limit or defeat ourselves. We use the Law in a negative manner.

Hans Christian Oersted, who discovered the relationship of electricity and magnetism, once said: "The Universe is a manifestation of an Infinite Reason and the laws of Nature are the thoughts of God." Just as the thought of God is the creative agency of the universe, and operates and functions through and as Law, so it is that our own thought is the creative agency in our experience. To change our lives we must start to think in a new way with new ideas.

Avoiding the Undesirable

The whole endeavor of man is to find freedom from bondage, freedom from those limitations with which he has surrounded himself. If he is sick, he wishes to be well; if he is impoverished, he wishes to live a more abundant life; if he is unhappy, he wants to live a life of joy and happiness; if he is afraid, he is trying either to escape through unconscious suicide or to find liberation from his fear through faith, a faith in something greater than he is.

We may safely say that the universe must be adequate; or, to put it another way, God does not make mistakes. Einstein is credited with saying that "God is subtle, but he is not malicious," and that "God does not play dice with the cosmos." It would follow then that God is neither unwhole, impoverished, limited, or unhappy and that our troubles must lie within ourselves. If bondage does not belong to God it must be a creation of man. We have a greater degree of choice and freedom than we have ever realized. In some way or other, by some inward compulsion and conviction, we feel that we were born to be free and happy and we ever desire to seek this larger life.

Of course we know that any freedom, to be true freedom, must be in accord with law. Therefore we must seek to find out just what is our individual relationship to this thing we call Life, or God, or the unseen Cause, or whatever term we have come to use to express the great Unknown, but not the great unknowable.

In searching out the nature of the great invisible Cause back of all things, that Principle which governs everything and which is also the Presence that flows in and through us, we are really discovering our relationship to God, and at the same time our relationship to each other, because we are all spiritual beings on the pathway of an eternal existence.

Would it be too much to say that whenever we discover something about the nature of God we shall also be discovering something about our own nature? Or, that in such degree as we discover what we *really* are we must be discovering what God is in us?

If it so happens, as we all are sure it must, that we belong to the Universe in which we live, and are some part of It, then it follows of necessity that no one can be either whole or happy until he discovers his *real* self. And if it so happens, as indeed it must, that one cannot discover his real self without finding his relationship to that which is greater than he is, then surely the pathway to freedom and wholeness lies in a conscious union with the invisible laws of Life and the great Intelligence behind them.

No man has a right to say he is not free, not free to think the way he chooses. It is true that over a great period of time he may have built barriers of limitation and restraint about the way he thinks, but these he was free to build or not to build. He is also free to remove them or augment them. We can easily see how others are limiting themselves in many respects by the way they have imprisoned their thinking. It is not so easy, however, to see the same thing in ourselves. If we would only have the courage really to look at our own way of thinking we would find that we have hampered and restricted ourselves no less than those about us. But once we discover this we are in a position to do something about it, we are ready to step out of our self-imprisonment. We are no longer captive to our negative thoughts but are free to hold our thoughts captive to our highest desire for good in our experience.

Don't Limit Yourself

Obvious illustrations of self-limitation are all about us. Does the man who "knows" he is always a failure ever become successful? What about the chronic invalid who always seems to revel in having everything in the medical book wrong with him—does he ever enjoy a healthy normal life? Or the person who feels sure that everyone is against him—does he find friendship, happiness, and joy in living? It can be said without much fear of contradiction that people reap what they sow, they experience what they think. Let us take a quick look at ourselves. In what ways are we experiencing what we feared, which the very process of fearful thought has brought to pass? Although it may be a very subtle thing to discover, in some way or other, whether we realize it or not, each thought possesses a creative force which in its cumulative effect is tremendous. A specific thought, even though entertained only once a day, can in the over-all picture be a powerful creative factor in any aspect of our experience.

For your own information it might be very enlightening to make a list of some of those things you think about a great deal which you *do not* want to happen to you. Then throw the list away. You do not want anything more to do with it. Its only purpose was to point out that in all probability you are not thinking as you should.

Think as You Please

We are free to think in any manner we desire; free to have our thoughts dwell on undesirable things we don't want, or good things we do want in health, affairs, and relationships. There is nothing in the nature of this world that forbids or prevents us from enjoying an ever-increasing amount of every good thing. It would have to be this way. For who has been able to discover that there is something in the nature of things which says a man must be unhappy? What could possibly say that one person has to be sick, or that another must be without friends? It is impossible to even comprehend such a thing as existing. If any man thinks it possible, then the God of his belief must also be sickly, unhappy, and sad. But with a firm conviction that there is One Mind, a supreme Intelligence, a spiritual Reality—God—that is whole, complete, and undivided against Itself, and both creates and is that which is created in accord with law and order, then we come to know that there is nothing in the nature of things against us, but that everything is for us. The only thing against us is ourselves—what we do to ourselves by the way we use our God-given freedom to think as we choose.

You Are Important

For the most part we have too low an opinion of ourselves. We need to place a new evaluation on ourselves. Not an evaluation which is blown up with conceit, but one which contains a sense of wonder, humility, and awe. We need to develop a deep sense of reverence for the Life that flows in and through us, and all things. For without It there would be nothing. We should have respect for ourselves, confidence in ourselves, and an assurance that all is right with us in our world. We but need let it be that way, for it is God's world, the creation of the One Intelligence, and as such it can never be in conflict with itself! With an increasing awareness of the fact that our mind is some part of the infinite Intelligence, we suddenly discover that we are more important than we thought.

Saying that man is an integral part of the Universe in no way implies that he is supposed to sit back and take life as he encounters it. Rather, we should think of man as partaking of the creativity of God, carving out his own future and destiny.

In learning to use the creative nature of our mind we are following a pathway which is both scientific and inspirational.

Scientific in that by entertaining spiritual and mental concepts we are not departing from law and order but increasingly coming to comply with them.

Inspirational in that every man longs to live a richer life, to express himself to the fullest, and to enjoy happiness and possess a sense of security.

4

YOUR NEW FREEDOM

> *He who floats with the current, who does not guide himself according to higher principles, who has no ideal, no conviction—such a man is a mere article of the world's furniture—a thing moved, instead of a living and moving being—an echo, not a voice. The man who has no inner life is the slave of his surroundings, as the barometer is the obedient servant of the air at rest, and the weathercock the humble servant of the air in motion.*
>
> —HENRI FREDERIC AMIEL

In RECENT YEARS we have heard much about affirmative prayer and positive thinking. It has been the subject of a great deal of conversation and has provided the basis for many books. However, it is regrettable that so much of what has been said or written has been interpreted as meaning that there should be nothing more than a Pollyanna attitude on the part of the individual. Nothing could be farther from the truth. Rightly approached, positive thinking does not mean an aggressiveness or the use of will power, but rather a dynamic, affirmative attitude toward life. The power and creativity that reside by nature in our thought are directed through the process of a prayer of faith which is based in the conviction that there must be a Wholeness back of everything. Constructive affirmative

positive thinking

thinking leads us to that Wholeness, and faith in that Wholeness is our key to the fruits of Its action.

Faith is a definite mental attitude which refuses to accept the opposite. Strangely enough, we already have such faith in most things in life. We believe that gravity will hold us in the position that we assume, and that a rock will fall when we release it from our hand. We believe that when we plant a garden it will grow. We believe that, through some process which we do not understand, the food we partake of will become converted into muscle and sinew, bone and blood. We are already living by faith and we don't know it! "The greatest thing which science does for us is to *reaffirm the reality of the Spirit*," is the conclusion of physicist Donald H. Andrews, as well as many other scientists. So we find that it is scientific to have a complete faith in that spiritual Reality which by the nature of things must be back of this world of ours.

We need to discard our old patterns of thought which have denied us the good we desire and brought upon us the woes and burdens we are carrying. We need to open up our minds, create new patterns of thinking, and discover and use the greater potentialities which reside at the center of our being.

Positive Thinking

It is most certain that the one who tries, who dares to think anew, who seeks to conform with the great laws of life, will soon discover that he is on the way to a fuller expression and experience of life. Since faith, faith in accord with reason, is but a certain way of thinking, we can all gradually change our mental attitudes from negative to positive, from fear to certainty, and discover that the Universe is for us and desires only that we succeed in all good things.

By assuming an affirmative attitude, by having our faith backed by reason, we will finally learn to control better what at first appear to be great negative influences in our lives. If day by day we are thinking better, things will be getting a

Proof: think positively, your life gets better.

little better. Then we will know that we are on the right road and all we have to do is to follow that road to its final destination. And in following that road we will find that we are proving for ourselves the reality of Spirit, and Its action as law and order.

No Big or Little

The action of any law is in no way concerned with size. The little rock will fall to the ground just as surely as the big one. The life that flows in the flea and the life that courses through the veins of the elephant is of the One Life. The same body of law applies to each. So it is with the Law of Mind, which cannot in any way be concerned with the size, importance, or supply of the good that we desire in our lives. We have to free ourselves from the habit of thinking in a small way, or that something may be too big or too good for us to experience. Our thoughts are the only limiting factors. The Law which responds to our thought is ready and able to accomplish all things.

Law

can accomplish all.

Experiment has enabled man to formulate many statements about the way certain laws operate and what they will accomplish. Just as the scientist has done in discovering the laws which govern the physical world, so we discover for ourselves, through our own experience, the nature of that Law which applies to our thought. And just as order exists in the physical world, so we are able to establish order and harmony in our experience, which at the present time may appear chaotic in comparison with what we would like it to be. In coming to discover the nature of any law, physical or mental, we find that it always remains intangible. We can find out "how" it works and the "way" it works, but never "why" it works. And as we find out more of the "how" and the "way" we are often confronted with the necessity of enlarging our concept of just what the law is. In commenting on the somewhat confused and complicated set of facts currently encountered in particle

We discover more of Law.

"how" not "why".

physics, J. Robert Oppenheimer, famed for his atomic research, feels that this is the result of being unable to see beyond the facts to the harmony which must exist behind them in terms of which they may be understood. Just as the scientist will never be able to exhaust the full meaning of what he has designated as law, so it is likely we will never be able completely to encompass the nature of the Law of Spirit or Mind. Who could encompass the creative Power of the Universe?

In considering the laws of the physical world, the men of science have been able for the most part to reduce to definite and specific mathematical equations the way they operate. It would be difficult to venture a guess as to whether such could be done with a spiritual or mental law, even though its operation is just as definite—if certain things are done certain results will occur. An expression of love brings a response of love; thoughts of hate will let one encounter only hate. These are definite and specific actions and reactions, but defining them in terms of formula or symbol is quite another thing. So perhaps any statement of the way such a law functions will of necessity be confined to explanation rather than mathematics, although it functions just as surely and accurately as any mathematically stated law.

In working out a new design for living logically and with a certitude that it will work, we need to remember it is based on the action of law and that the success of it will be determined by the level of our understanding of this action. Our experience is the result of the automatic reaction of law upon our thought, whether it relates to our physical health, our relationships with others, or just the sheer joy of living. But the action is a response to the *totality* of our thought, past and present.

You Are Not in Pieces

Body, mind, and spirit are not separated, isolated parts of life. They are a unity. We merely call different aspects of this unity by different names. Our mind is not separated from our body. Our body is not separate from that infinite Intelligence which created it, neither is our mind apart from the One Mind or Spirit. They are expressions of one great Whole, which is active in them. Just as it is the mission of science to discover one law which includes other basic physical laws, so also it is man's endeavor to realize that there is an all-inclusive spiritual Reality which resides within us, and nothing about us is not subject to Its creative activity.

One might ask: Even if our minds do partake of the creative nature of the infinite Mind or Spirit, is there not by nature a limitation to this creative action in our experience? Of course there is a limitation—not one that exists naturally, but one we have imposed upon ourselves. We can only use what we know. The more we understand, the more we will be able to accomplish. This holds true in any form of endeavor. Any invention has always been a possibility. The universe has not become more than it was before. Rather, there has been an increased knowledge and understanding on the part of man as to the nature of what resides in the universe, resulting in his being able to make the new invention possible. The same holds true of all discoveries in the past and those to come in the future. The more we come to learn and know about the world we live in, the more we will be able to use and direct the inherent limitless possibilities of nature to bring about greater wonders.

Does this not also apply to our use of the creative nature of our own thought? The more we come to realize the nature of God and our relationship with God, the more we will be able to comply with the real nature of things as they are, and constructively direct our lives into greater good. Any limitation which may appear to be barring us from a greater experience of good, we may be sure, is a limitation we have placed upon ourselves.

Mental Housecleaning

Such limitations as we may have made for ourselves need to be removed to the best of our ability. We need to work at clearing away those thoughts, ideas, or concepts which appear to be barriers to the greater good we desire. We have to grow and expand to break the confines of our own imprisonment, whether it be of our own individual thinking or the limitations of the thinking in the world about us that we have accepted. No progress was ever made by the individual who was satisfied with the *status quo*.

Old ways of thinking are not good enough for us. If they were, where might we find ourselves? Living in a mud hut, wearing animal skins for clothing? And what before that? This may sound ridiculous, but at what point could we possibly say that yesterday was good enough? What yesterday? They go back to the beginning of man. It is to the future that we must look. To increased wisdom and understanding. To greater awareness of the nature of the world we live in. To fuller realization of the fact that we are a creation and activity of infinite Intelligence. Such a realization is something that is never fully achieved but is a continuing thing, becoming bigger, broader, and greater.

And as we learn to do this we shall discover for ourselves that just as the many wonders of electronics and engineering were always inherent in the universe, so there is also inherent in the universe the potential for the greater good we desire. Upon this knowledge, supported by unwavering faith and conviction that this potential does reside in the nature of life, we shall start to think anew, to plan a more joyous life.

You Don't Forget

There are some aspects of man's mind that we have not mentioned. When we speak of our *mind* we usually refer to

our mind

that activity of it which constitutes our everyday mode of thought; the process of thinking, of ascertaining the condition of the world about us through our senses, our self-knowingness or consciousness. Another aspect of our mind may be referred to as the subconscious or deeper realm which contains all we have thought, felt, and experienced. At the subconscious level is also centered an intelligent activity of life that automatically beats our hearts, circulates our blood, fills our lungs, focuses our eyes, and directs all processes of assimilation, elimination, and circulation.

We have said that our total thought content creates our experiences. This means the sum total of both conscious thought and thought which has been stored in the subconscious as memory. Inasmuch as there is no volition, no initiative in the subconscious, we find that it is subject to the conscious mind; it takes directions from it, believes all that is passed on to it. It does not reason, it reacts. And because the subconscious holds more in storage than the conscious mind can ever entertain at one time, we see that what we experience through the creative nature of our thought is mostly determined by the larger content of the subconscious. From one point of view it might appear that the subconscious is more important than the conscious, but on the other hand we find that it is neither more important nor less important.

memory in subconscious

One task which confronts the individual is to learn to control the content of the subconscious. However, this does not mean to manhandle it, fight it, or look upon it as an enemy. Rather, we should consider it as an obedient servant, plastic and willing, ready and waiting, dynamic and certain in its acceptance of ideas we implant in it. When we are able to give it a proper content, through constructive thinking, we shall find that our total thought content will so change that the same law which may now bind us will provide us with a greater freedom—freedom from want, illness, and unhappiness.

subcons. = servant accepts our thoughts

It is interesting to note that throughout history the great thinkers have come to realize that Life Itself is an infinite

Thinker—God—whose thoughts operate as Law producing and maintaining the physical universe. We find that the same thing occurs in our own lives; the entire body of our thought, that which we are now consciously thinking as well as that which is stored in our subconscious, acts as the law of our experience. Once we come to know the manner in which thought, past and present, acts as law, we can forget any explanation of its operation and merely endeavor to so guide our thinking that the sum total of our thought will be on the plus side, providing desirable results.

our thought is our law of experience.

so guide it.

As we become aware of the fact that we are confronted by no limitations other than the ones we set for ourselves, this does not mean that we have the power to command the revolutions of the planets, or set the mountains in their places, or create the oceans and the rivers. But we *can* control our actions and reactions in and to life. In our personal world of experience we are certainly given the privilege to be happy or unhappy, to be whole or incomplete.

we can control our thoughts

You Are Always Creative

There is never an end of the Infinite's creative action. Similarly we are always creative, consciously or unconsciously, in our world of experience. This we need always to remember. We are always creative, but is what we are creating what we most desire? There is also another aspect to creativity which resides at the center of us. *Life in us always needs to be expressed.* Once we cease to find constructive outlets for Its flow in and through us, we block Its action in every phase of living and we begin to fall apart mentally, emotionally, and physically.

creativity

What are some examples in everyday experience which demonstrate the way a pattern of thinking acts as a law of life? We notice that the proverbial grouch has a very difficult time being joyous and happy. Smoking and drinking are laws that we establish for ourselves. Chronic constipation, a fluttering heart, or nervous twitching of facial muscles are indications of the

we create

way patterns of thought have disrupted the normal activities of the laws which control and direct the functioning of our body at the autonomic level.

Three Phases of Creativity

(handwritten: (what) (how) Spirit — law — result 1 2 3)

No matter in which direction we may look, we will always find three steps, stages, or phases of creativity. We find that (1) there is Spirit, Consciousness, Mind, or Intelligence, (2) which, functioning through and as Law, (3) evidences Itself as the substance of experience. It is interesting to note that many of the outstanding theoretical physicists of today consider *form* to be the all-important thing in their investigation of the physical world. Erwin Schrödinger, one of the most brilliant of contemporary theoretical physicists who was awarded the Nobel Prize for his work on *wave mechanics,* feels that form, not substance, is the essence of things. "The *new* idea is that what is permanent in . . . ultimate particles . . . is their shape and organization." What is it that creates the form, that determines the shape and nature of any thing? This they say is in the realm of the intangible, the invisible. This thing of thought, the spiritual, may be the source of new forms to be filled by substance in accord with law.

There is no reason whatsoever not to believe that the same sequence of creativity exists for us in our lives. We think. Our thought operating through law becomes our experience. Our thought creates the form or pattern which is the mold of the substance of our experience.

Discover a New Freedom

(handwritten: Deduce intelligent creator)

The mere fact that purpose, form, shape, and organization do exist implies that there must be *something* which created or established them. This would of necessity mean that such a creative factor would have to be intelligent, for the action of law is intelligent. At the same time we cannot imagine such a creative Intelligence being other than *conscious,* for if It were not conscious that would mean that the Creator of the universe would be less than that which It creates, which would be impossible. The myriad forms and patterns evident in all things show us that they are not the whimsy of chance but are the result of the action and interaction of inviolable law in response to the directive ideas of a conscious Intelligence.

So we find that in saying there is one creative Intelligence back of all things we are entirely in accord with what many of the outstanding scientific minds of our day are also saying, and also with what the wise and the learned have been saying for ages.

This Mind is also the One Presence in which all things exist, and the One Intelligence which all people use. From a seashell, to a blade of grass, to the consciousness of man, we find one grand succession—Intelligence unfolding Itself in and as Its creation through the creative medium of Law. All this may be summed up as the Principle of Life.

We are some part of this system, for there is nothing else for us to be part of. And within each there resides an *interior awareness* which knows this to be true, which knows itself to be some part of that greater whole. We shall discover it if we look within ourselves, not outside. And from this there springs in each of us that inborn faith which enables us to know there is Intelligence and Law in the universe, and to understand that there must be a few simple rules which, if followed, will enable us to comply with the nature of things as they are and lead us to success, happiness, and wholeness.

While it is true that some have had a faith which most people do not possess, it is not true that others may not acquire the same faith. Certainly we have every reason to suppose that we could go far beyond our present experience, and through faith and conviction find a new freedom in life. We should feel that this is a normal and natural activity of our innermost nature which we are attempting to discover fully.

The path we seek to follow is the same path followed in all

scientific research, which is a constant search into nature in an attempt to discover the laws that control its action, so that they may be complied with and used. When we realize that our experiences are based on laws just as definite as physical laws, and having the same source, we will overcome both superstition and timidity. We will have found that the deep fundamental laws of our being are laws of thought. This means that our thought acts upon something, or that something acts in accordance with the way we think, so that there are specific, tangible, and measurable results. Using this action of thought for our greater good means simply that we are bringing our lives into conformity with the fundamental nature of Life—God.

We are aware of ourselves as having consciousness, intelligence, and the ability to think.

Our minds did not appear from nowhere so must have some source.

This source must of necessity be similar to its expression.

We find that our minds are related to the One Mind.

Infinite Mind has become individualized within us as our mind.

Our mind partakes of the creativeness of infinite Mind and we may direct this creativity in our experience at the level of our understanding of it.

5
CHANGES
ARE NECESSARY

As rivers have their source in some far off fountain, so the human spirit has its source. To find his fountain of spirit is to learn the secret of heaven and earth.

—LAO-TZU

WE ARE ALL living in a world of continual change, a world in which thought, thing, and experience are all in a constant state of flux. It is the very nature of the universe that there should be continual change and variation. It is a living world, the creation of a living creative Intelligence, not a static world created by a God now dead or departed who has left it to decay. No. It is vital and alive. The Mind that created it is not apart from it, but is always active in and through it.

But behind that which changes, behind that which causes the change, we have found that there is something stable and changeless. Something eternal upon which all of the external events depend for their very existence. Behind the endless process of change and the infinite variety of experience and expression there is That which does not change.

We should never be afraid of change, never fearful of what will come. Instead we should bring to bear on each new event the influence of the creative nature of our thought—an influence that is founded on an inward calm, a sense of certainty and peace, which will reflect itself in the changing scene of our everyday lives.

As we look for and discover the nature of the Infinite which does not change, we find that we develop a complete trust in the integrity of It. We are again reminded of Einstein's remark that "God does not play dice with the cosmos." And we then come to possess a feeling of security which is enhanced by the knowledge that each of us has a personal and intimate relationship with the Infinite. It is from this inward basis of certainty—this sense and awareness of our relationship to God, who is changeless but from whom flow infinite expressions— that all our thoughts should flow.

Total integrity of principle

Infinite Variety

In our daily living we encounter infinite variety in all things. But behind the expression there is the pattern or form which is the foundation. There is a unity but not a uniformity that exists between all similar expressions. A unity that resides in the ultimate creative nature of the Universe; a unity that allows freedom of individual expression.

unity but not uniformity

An obvious lesson can be learned if we look at ourselves, our families, our friends. We discover we are all human beings, all pretty much the same. A head, two eyes, two ears, a nose, mouth, body, arms, and legs. And as we look farther afield at the entire human race, we find some races are tall, others short; some white, others black, yellow, or red. But behind every man, every race, there is the basic pattern, a pattern that is individually expressed.

Basic pattern for humans

If there were not the possibility of variation of expression, Life could never have developed Its infinite variety. And if there had not been behind the development of man a basic pattern for man there never would have been any way for him to develop.

The Great Explosion

One of the most amazing events in the development of man into his present physical form occurred in the early stages of his existence. According to anthropologist Loren Eiseley, man at that time, in physical structure and general appearance, gave evidence of the man that was to be. The pattern existed. But through infinite changes and variations a fuller and more perfect expression of it occurred. Then an amazing thing happened. For no reason that the scientists have been able to determine, man developed an enlarged brain. A brain far beyond the capacity needed for the containment of cells necessary for the operation of the senses for survival and the automatic functioning of the physical body. Without any previous indication, without any comparable thing occurring elsewhere in any living thing, man suddenly (in terms of geological time) possessed a brain that was capable of functioning far beyond any demands that could ever be made on it by the physical body. *It was an elaborate instrument that was capable of being a channel for thought, creative thought.*

Why did it appear? What caused it to appear? What was its purpose? There is no academic answer forthcoming through the strict limitations science places upon itself. But those who have devoted their lives to science sometimes step outside their laboratories, for a moment turn aside from their microscopes, and say what they think.

Freedom from Domination

Some of them say that with the advent of this unpredictable development in man something new appears to have been injected into God's creation. Something different had been brought into creation by the Mind behind all creation—a unique expression of Itself. Thus man was freed from many of the instinctive limitations of his physical body. He was aware

Aware!

of himself! He could think! Infinite Mind is the only thing that
can be ascertained to have thought, consciousness, and intelligence, and now It established for Itself in and through man
a means of awareness, creativeness, and consciousness of what
It had created. With the development of the larger brain in
man, Mind came forth anew into Its creation, ushering in a
whole new era, the future of which we but little realize. We
now need to learn to free ourselves from the complete domination of the instinctive functioning of the nervous system, although it serves our physical body well and has brought it to
the high degree of perfection which it now exhibits.

The physical body has always faced a threat in one of two
ways: either to fight, or to escape through flight. This same
instinctive reaction is of value to man today, but he needs to
place a limitation on its action. Man deals largely with ideas
in his daily life, and when he encounters one that he does
not like his body is whipped up to engage itself in combat with
it, or is prepared for flight from it. Even though the body is
never able actually to do anything about either fighting or
fleeing from an idea, the wear and tear that results in it are
most disastrous.

phys.— fight or flight.

we still react same way.

We now need to discover that new thing which resides within
us and is ever seeking fuller expression through us, and we
shall find that it is the individualization in us of the infinite
conscious creative Intelligence.

Nonresistance

We generally seem to resist change, even that which is better
for us. We also appear to resist being what we really are. We
need to learn carefully and surely to permit ourselves to accept
the fuller expression of the Mind that is within us. Against
this there must be no resistance. For in Its creative flow through
us rests our entire future—the greater person we may be, and
the richer life we desire to enjoy.

We have to learn to PERMIT ourselves to express God.

When we establish within our thought a nonresistance to

We are a part of something never affected by change.

that Power which is greater than we are, we are at the same time accepting within ourselves a stability that is the stability of the Universe. We find ourselves secure, for we know that we are part of That which causes change but is never affected by any of the changes. As we gradually attain this sense of security we will find that we view the changes that occur about us in a proper perspective. We will have stopped letting ourselves be blown about like a straw in the wind, or tossed helplessly about in a turbulent sea whose waves are doubt and fear and anxiety.

atom has stable center.

We may liken ourselves to the atom, whose center or nucleus is stable. Around it revolve the electrons in orderly, harmonious orbits. In much the same way, once we discover the stable center that resides within us, we may have all our experiences revolve around us in an orderly way. Once our consciousness becomes stabilized through security founded on a conviction of the nature of God, and we come to have an inner awareness that the Creative Intelligence of the Universe is also what resides at the center of us, then will our experiences take on a pattern of harmony—a natural outflowing of our inner security.

Learn to Live

We need to express, to create

The whole purpose of our lives is to *live* Life. Life is not to be avoided. There is no need to feel that one should forego any beneficial pleasure or joy in living. It would appear that there is a need for us to express creatively the Infinite residing at the center of us. Inasmuch as nothing is big or small to God we could in turn say that nothing is big or small in our own lives, and enter as joyously into what we call the small things of life as into what we call the larger things, for they are all a part of the whole pattern of living.

Not selfish

There is no trace of selfishness in our desire to experience greater happiness, health, and abundance, even though through ignorance some might say there is. They would be the ones who would cut themselves off from the sunlight, feeling that to

stand in its full light would deprive someone else of its benefit. Or they would take only a quick glance at a beautiful sunset or at the stars in the heavens for fear there would not be
enough left for another to look at. No one in experiencing
health, happiness, or abundance of any kind need feel that he in
any way deprives another. The source of them all is limitless.
All we are doing in seeking a greater expression of them in
our lives is permitting a fuller expression of Life Itself in and
through us, and It can never deprive Itself of anything. This
does not mean that we can deliberately and intentionally try to
attain our good by taking from another. If we seek to deprive
another, we also deprive ourselves. What we desire for ourselves we must also desire for others; then the experience of all
is enriched.

When we do this we find that we have consciously used our
thought in a creative manner. Instead of feebly grasping and
struggling for tangible, changeable effects, we are at that creative place from which the desired effects emanate. We are at
the ever-flowing spring, the source of life-giving water, not
squabbling in the market place over the scarcity of a cup of
stale water.

In speaking of our daily activities we need to keep firmly
in mind that what we experience in our affairs and relationships is no less a reality than anything else in the physical
world. They are just as real as the chair we are sitting on. And
both originate in the same manner, a result of the creative
nature of thought.

We should develop the practice of communing daily with
the Spirit that resides within us. And such a communion should
be based on a deep inward sense of belonging to Life, of being
a part of It, of trusting It and having confidence in It, and of
knowing that as we do so the future is certain in such degree
as we make the present a time of joy, of happiness, of peace,
and of good will toward others.

These are not merely sweet-sounding words; rather they point
to the very center of Being Itself, which is an infinite harmony

pervading everything and finding fulfillment in a limitless activity. As we express the fundamental needs of life—to live, to be creative, to be happy, to be whole, and to join with others in a community of spirit, of thought and purpose and endeavor—we make our lives and the lives of those about us things of fulfillment and joy.

Life Is What You Make It

The two fundamental propositions which we must remember are that we are creative centers in Mind, and that our thought is creative through the action of a Power greater than we are. If these propositions are true it follows that everything in our personal experience depends upon our mental and emotional reactions to life, and our deep realization of the intimate relationship we have with the Infinite.

In this way we see that life is what we make it and there are tremendous possibilities implied; but at the same time this seems to place a great responsibility on our shoulders that we do not always desire to recognize or accept, regardless of the potentials involved. For the most part we seem to want to shun responsibility, we want to do things the easy way, we would like to just coast along and have everything taken care of for us. However, we have outgrown our crib and we have spread our wings and are on our own, both in our own physical lives and in the life of the race of man on earth. We are maturing and in so doing we cannot evade or ignore the nature of things as they are. We do think, our thought is creative, and as a result our life is what we make it. It is a case of sink or swim. And there is something within us that does not want us to sink, so we learn to swim although our first efforts may appear feeble. Where previously we may have frantically splashed around getting nowhere, barely keeping our heads above water, we now know that swim we can, and swim we will, carrying ourselves along the stream of life with direction and confidence.

The Endless Challenge

We need not be the least bit fearful of the fact that life is what we make it. For this is the great challenge, the endless opportunity, and our God-given privilege. All we have to do is to learn how to go about making our life better. The initiative rests with us. We have to do something about it; if we don't we just continue to coast along in the same old hectic muddle, bemoaning our lot. And *we* have to do it, nobody else can do it for us. We do our own thinking and we do our own living, and the two cannot be separated. There is no way that it can be done by proxy, as much as we might at times wish this were possible.

Through the process of our thinking we are either repelling or attracting the life we want to live. It is not only the individual thought that does this to us, important as it is, but the total content of our thought. The idle wish or the passing desire that life should be better will not make it better, when our thought during the day is otherwise taken up with intense concentration on and absorption with the utterly deplorable conditions and circumstances in which we may find ourselves— a situation which we eventually discover we have assiduously created for ourselves.

Making our life what it is or what we desire it to be rests in the nature of all our thought, conscious as well as subconscious. It is for this reason that if we are to have a better life there has to be consistency, definiteness, and continuous thinking along a certain line and in a specific direction. Not once a day, but all day. Otherwise you will discover that your thinking has wavered and changed so much, you have negated your own thinking so often, that in the total at the end of the day the good has been entirely canceled out and you want nothing to do with what you have left.

But you can start right now to make a life that is new and

more to your liking. What you are going to add up today will probably have a few more plus signs and a few less minus signs than yesterday, and tomorrow will be even better than today. And as the plus signs become more numerous in your thinking you will never have to bother to count them, for they will be appearing all about you as the plus experiences, the good things, in the new life you are making for yourself.

Make Some Changes

It is wonderful to know that through this simple activity of directed thinking we can gradually shift around the whole basis and nature of our thought content and thought habits to a point that is more favorable for us.

Even though there may be stored away in the subconscious many years of negative thinking along certain lines, this in no way need concern us. In fact, we do not even need to bother ourselves with what may or may not be there. What we need to do is to start today to make sure that the content of our conscious thought is good, and think clearly and definitely about it. What occurs then is similar to drops of clear water falling into a glass of murky, inky water. Not much appears to have changed with the first drop, but slowly and surely the water in the glass becomes clearer and clearer until it is as clear as the drops that fall into it. New plus patterns of thinking will gradually supplant undesirable ones of long standing. But we have to make sure our thought has a *plus* pattern.

Life is what we make it, thought by thought. Whenever we have reached that point where we don't like what we have made, we are tired of what we have been going through, we want no more of it, then we can wake up to the fact that we may make it any way we want. Where we in our ignorance may have made a sorry mess of things, we may now efficiently, with purpose and calculated design, create a new experience in living. We may consciously induce those new patterns of thought which we wish to become permanent and continually creative in our lives.

All this is not done by holding thoughts by concentration or by willing, but by the gentle and more powerful influence of persistent and consistent affirmation, which gradually changes the old into the new. Our experience will soon show us that the new is coming to pass.

The purpose of our lives is to live Life.

Do not shy away from It, be fearful of It, or deprive yourself of Its full enjoyment.

The sooner we come to realize the full nature of Life, the sooner we will be able to accept and experience Its innate goodness in all that we are and do.

Our lives are what we make them, thought by thought, and herein lies the possibility to express creatively and partake of the Divinity that is at the center of us.

6 GREAT POSSIBILITIES

Courage, then, for God works in you. In order of time you embody in outer acts what is for him the truth of his eternity.
—JOSIAH ROYCE

CAUSE AND EFFECT are terms which are usually associated with the fields of physical science, but there is no reason why they may not be applied to other fields as well. The implication in the terms is that when something is done, something else results, and that there is a definite relationship between the two. When you turn the switch, the light comes on. When you turn the handle of the faucet, water flows. The light switch does not provide a flow of water, neither does the faucet handle provide light. For each cause in whatever realm there is an effect which is related to and proceeds directly from the cause. We say "in whatever realm." This means not only in all fields of science but also in the realms of mind and spirit. It means cause and effect also applies in all our activities and relationships. At some point or other, in some way or other, because the universe is a unity, there is a relationship of cause and effect between all things regardless of their nature.

The original cause of the universe according to the Bible was a thought in the Mind of God. Everything that exists was first an idea, and it is the nature of ideas to take form. Some people say that they believe this because it is in the Bible. To others it appears as a logical necessity to account for things as they are. Many cosmogonists and astronomers who seek to determine the nature of the universe as a whole feel that at one time about four billion years ago there was a somewhat quiescent mass of tightly compressed particles, those particles out of which atoms are built. Then something happened. And within a very short time, a very explosive time, physical creation began and is still continuing according to inherent patterns which would have had to exist prior to that original explosive moment. "God said." Mind thought. Is there a difference? There was a cause and there was an effect. And that original causative factor did not cease to be, but is active causation still creating effects. It is without beginning and without end. Pure Mind knows no limitations.

Creation still going on.

Astronomer Gustaf Stromberg has written much on this subject and has said that when the physical world of space, time, and energy was yet unborn something far more important existed. This was Mind, Cosmic Mind, or World Soul, which *was* and *is* the source of all things physical as well as the ultimate origin of our minds.

Proving a Theory

Let us turn from the cosmos to a seed. There is not much difference theoretically, in spite of appearances. We consciously plant a seed in the ground. What happens? According to a law of nature there is unfoldment of the seed into a definite form, and always a form which is the outward manifestation of an invisible inner pattern. Applying the same process to a thought, we find that according to a law in nature the thought develops into a condition or experience which is a complete embodiment of the concept or idea contained in the thought. We come to the conclusion that our whole experience in life is but the unfolding of ideas that have consciously or unconsciously been entertained by us.

seed

invisible inner pattern

thought

If we take this as the key in our use of cause and effect we

shall see that the starting point, so far as we are concerned in
designing a new life, is to shift the whole basis of our thought
from the belief we are controlled by outward circumstances,
and enslaved by them, to a realization that the same creative
Spirit that made everything, that is the Cause of everything, is
at the center of our being in all Its fullness.

All this perhaps sounds like a very wonderful theory, but
does it work? It is just like any other theory, it will remain
a theory until it is proved. The proof of any truth rests only
in our practical use of it. And each individual must prove
this theory for himself in his own life and experience. Others
may just *say* it works, but we can discover evidence that it *does*
work. But it will not work of its own accord. Each has to make
it work for himself. We have to demonstrate in our lives that
we are actually dealing with and using the ultimate Causative
Force, that we are individualizations of the universal Spirit,
and that we are using universal Law.

The Law of Correspondence

Our purpose in affirmative prayer, spiritual mind treatment,
or right thinking is to stabilize our own thought, to think
clearly; always understanding that all things are possible to that
Power greater than we are. Equally important is the knowledge
that this Power can do for us only what It does through us;
that there is something which actually brings about conditions,
circumstances, and situations that correspond to our mental
attitudes. This could be called a law of correspondence, the
outer manifestation corresponding to the inner thought. The
relationship between the effect and its cause, between what
thought produces and what it is. It is the law illustrated in this
Biblical passage: "And the Word was made flesh, and dwelt
among us. . . ."

This does not mean that we sit around all day thinking profoundly, pushing ponderous abstract ideas about, which to say
the least is exhausting. This is exactly what we want to avoid.

We must never make the designing of a new life a labor, for if we do it will lose its vitality and spontaneity, and the effort involved will become just another burden we have to tolerate and subject ourselves to. What we do has to be something we want to do for the sheer joy of doing it. Only then will proper results be forthcoming.

What we are doing in our undertaking is to experiment with the greatest Principle ever discovered by man, which, even though It is infinite, is personal to each one of us; which because It knows neither big nor little, hard nor easy, will flow with equal force and power through the individual use we make of It.

Using Ideas

As we start using the idea of cause and effect, start experimenting with the relationship of thought and experience, it will not be long before we will have established for ourselves the validity of the theory. Then we will no longer be interested in proving the theory, but will accept it and use it to the limit of our ability. It may be some seemingly little thing that will clear our minds of any doubt, or perhaps it will be something big. It doesn't matter what the proof may be, the process is the same, and big or little has no significance. A parking space. So important at times. Why do some people always seem to find one just where they want it? They want one, they need one, they know one will be available at the right place at the right time. It is usually there, and quite often we have been a passenger as the car pulled into it. Nothing ponderous about this. Just a calm assurance, complete confidence. They *know* the parking place will be there. Simple. Almost too simple? What is the reason? Cause and effect. Thought becoming thing or situation.

One of the worst pitfalls we could find ourselves in is spending all our time theorizing how *this* can become *that*, trying to determine all the various relationships that exist between different kinds of causes and various types of effects. At some point every science student has to take his nose out of the textbook and go into the laboratory and experimentally prove for himself that the theories he has read about are true. So it is with each of us. The only way for us to prove that a theory we believe in is correct is to set our reading aside and start doing. With the conviction that the theory is right, start experimenting and the results will be forthcoming. Then we will begin to experience the best days of our lives. We might start by smiling at a person we have always ignored or glowered at. We'll be surprised at the effects which result from this cause. Silly? Insignificant? No, how powerful! And so much worthwhile.

Cause and effect always works, and there is nothing too big or too little for it to cope with.

You Have No Alibis

It seems that in almost every aspect of our experience we find ourselves limited in some way or another. We find that we are blocked at some point beyond which we are unable to go. Whether this applies to a fuller enjoyment of health, greater success, or better relationships, does not matter. All of us encounter certain blocks or limitations at some point, but the point at which they appear is different for each individual. Some people are never well, others are always poor. It doesn't appear as though they ever got started living a decent life. They really have limitations! But why any limitations?

One of the most difficult things for us to believe, or convince ourselves of, is that the only limitations we have are the ones we have created for ourselves. That it is we who have cluttered up our lives. It is as though we spent all our time gathering up limitations, placing them as roadblocks on our pathway, then grumbling about the fact that they block our way.

Where do they come from? Thought and thing. What causes

them to occur? Cause and effect. There is no other way they could become a part of our experience. There is nothing in the nature of things, in Mind, which would permit the fullness of life and living in one person and place restrictions and limitations on another. We have no place to turn for an alibi, we are confronted with the unpleasant task of looking at ourselves in a mirror and pointing at ourselves with an accusing finger, saying, "You did it!" Of course we will deny it. We will ignore the accusation. We will try every means of logic and reason at our disposal to dismiss the charge. But there will be something deep inside that knows it is true, and also knows that something can be done about it.

The limitations we find encircling us have but one source—they spring from our thought. They are the result of our negative habitual thought patterns, conscious or tucked away in the subconscious, which may have been instigated by our past experiences or the blind acceptance of what now appear to be the wrong ideas and concepts of others.

An engineer involved in the construction of vehicles for travel in outer space said in effect that there is nothing in nature which in any way places any limitation on man's thought or what he can do. Right now we can let our thought go to any place on earth, or in the heavens; our thought can move to any place in time; we can envision any of all possible situations. Our mind is free. Why don't we let it free our experience, not confine it? Why not let it create for us what we desire and not bar us from our greater good?

But for our thought to create freedom and not limitation for us, we must fully realize its nature, what it is, how it works, and the way to use it. Our new design for living cannot be built in a haphazard way; this kind of building we have already done too much of, with undesirable results. We conscientiously move forward step by step, idea by idea, and as we do so we find we are able to remove limitations which may now exist and make certain no new ones are established.

Are You Asking for Trouble?

Where and how do some of our limitations come into existence? Many are obvious, in fact so obvious that we seldom see them. Others may evade our search for some time. Who is the person who has the most colds during the winter? The person who knows he is going to have them. Who is first to have the new ailment that seems to be going the rounds? The one who hears of it first and starts looking for all the symptoms. It is so simple to limit our experience of health. And quite often there is a choice to be made as to what appears to be the lesser of two evils. Doctors have discovered that there is no physical reason for children to evidence a higher percentage of legitimate colds on a Monday morning than any other morning of the week. Yet it is Monday morning the cold makes its appearance. The suffering caused by the cold apparently is less than that encountered at school. In such instances the limitation is consciously imposed. This could make us wonder considerably about what we are consciously doing to ourselves. How often do we intentionally get sick, invite illness and disease, to avoid or escape another situation?

Then there is the bank account. For too many people it is so small that it is hardly worth talking about. But regardless of that, it is of utmost importance in more ways than one. Our earned income that goes into it represents what our worth is to the rest of the world, what service in some way we have been able to render others. The amount in the account of itself means little, what passes through the account is what is important. Money is to be used in one way or another. However, more often than not, people seem to have a fixed idea in their minds that there will never be more than $10, $100, $1,000, or $10,000, as the case may be, in the account for them to use. And for some reason or other there is never more than that amount! The same applies to one's earning capacity. People seem to get a feeling of being "stuck" or pegged at a certain salary figure, commission level, or volume of profit in a business. And there the situation stays. Quite often goals are set up for the standard of living or income desired. This is fine and needed. But once the goal is reached we need to be sure to establish another, or else the first goal becomes a limiting factor on any future accomplishment. In fact that first goal may have been so firmly implanted in our way of thought that it will be a little difficult to supplant it.

Don't Say "Can't"

Limitations are always easy to establish, in fact too easy. Every time we reflect on our inability to do or accomplish something we are setting up an increased barrier to the doing or accomplishing. Every time we have an alibi for undesirable results we may have achieved, we firmly establish that alibi as the limiting factor for our future activity. Every way we turn we find that for the most part we are spending our time setting up and maintaining limitations rather than removing them and moving ahead free and unrestricted. We have been using the limitless potential of the power of thought to impose limitations in every aspect of our living. Is it any wonder that our old design for living was far from adequate? Created in a careless manner, it contained so many ideas about the good things in life we could *not* have that there was very little space left for the good things we could have. We have filled our lives with too many "can'ts."

The person who is able to free his thought from the dominance of the past, from confining self-imposed restrictions as to what and how he will think, who places no barriers on the good today will bring him, is the one who is able to live a creative life. His thought is unlimited and so is his experience. And at the same time he accepts, without restriction, the flow and activity of Mind in and through him.

From such people have come all the great accomplishments of mankind. Discovery of the secrets of nature, the great works of art, great books, poetry, and music, the inventions and ways to use the raw materials of the physical world. The wise and thoughtful never have placed limitations or restrictions on themselves in their particular field of endeavor. Their thought was free of the past, free of the present. They accepted a creativity which expressed through them in such a manner as to bring forth that which was fresh and new, thus marking the milestones in the ability of man to bring into tangible experience more of the limitless potential which resides at the center of his own mind and consciousness—a focal point of the activity of God, Mind, or Spirit.

At this point a person might say, "I don't see how all this works or how I could possibly use it." This is a normal reaction, and a familiar type of expression. But by saying it and thinking it, what is he doing to himself? First there is the idea involved that he will never understand it, and that he will never be able to use it. So what happens? He never will understand or be able to use it! He will be barring himself from the positive and constructive use of the power of thought; he actually will be using it, without knowing it, in a destructive manner. Then there is that part of his statement, "I don't see." What is the result of that? The obvious thing, of course. His faculty of vision is gradually diminished. A not infrequent occurrence in psychosomatic medical cases.

Start to Accept Life

In one respect it is sad but true that our limitations originate within ourselves. But on the other hand it is perhaps the most wonderful thing that could happen. For now we are not dealing with something over which we have no control, but instead we are dealing with that over which we can have complete control, our thought. To do something about limitations we do not need to wait until tomorrow to start. Today is the day. Start right now. But we may feel that we have too many problems, too many worries and aches and pains to get under way. Alibis. The more difficulties we may feel we have, the more imperative it is that we start to do something about them right now, rather than indulge in creating more difficulties. But we just can't find the time to start to think in a new way, to start to create a new design for living. Alibi again. We never will *find* the time, we must *take* the time. If anything is to be done at all, now is the time to start. No doubt we have been and are now thinking in ways that are destructive of our good. We didn't have to make undue effort to do this. Neither will the other way of thinking, the constructive way, require undue effort. We just start doing it, and once we start it will become a normal and natural process. As a result our lives will begin to become more normal and natural, more in accord with the nature of things as they really are.

Nothing is more certain than that we have entertained too much morbidity and doubt and fear when it comes to thinking of God, Mind, and our relationship to Life. We have imposed the limitations of our own thought on the flow of Its activity in us. We have limited our experience of Life Itself by what we consider Life to be. We are neatly caught in a trap of our own creation. As we limit God, or the activity of Mind through us, we are limiting ourselves. If we say God can and will only provide us with a certain degree of health and happiness, then we can never have more than the degree we believe in. We can never limit the nature of the Infinite, but we can limit our experience of It by our limited concept of It. Many feel that God intended them to have a life of suffering and hardship, and is it any wonder that that is what they have?

This way of thinking is a sign of spiritual infantilism and intellectual starvation and belongs only to those who are afraid of God and the reality of their own being. We need to know that there is no limitation in the Mind that created all, and that there is no necessity for us to limit ourselves in any way. We must strike out boldly in creating our new design for living by enlarging our sphere of thinking, thereby increasing our range of experience and degree of fulfillment of the good life.

Man as a self-conscious expression of Spirit, which is never limited, encounters limitations only through his own thinking.

Man imposes limitations on himself through wrong thinking.

We must wake up to the tremendous creative nature of our thought.

We can specifically, definitely, direct our thinking in such a way as to be productive of good in our experience.

7
DISCOVERING YOURSELF

In God are present: power, which is the source of everything; knowledge, which contains the details of the ideas; and, finally, will, which changes or produces things in accordance with the principle of the greatest good.

—LEIBNITZ

EMERSON SAID he awaited the advent of anyone who would liken all the laws of nature to laws of thought. This wisest of Americans and one of the greatest thinkers of any age felt that the laws of mind must work with the same consistency and accuracy as the laws of physics or the laws of any of the exact sciences. In the period in which he wrote there seemed no likelihood that this was possible except in the realm of speculative thought, which at that time had little or no place in the fields of science.

But times have changed. We have learned more about the nature of the world we live in during the past hundred years than during man's entire previous history. And during the past hundred years, or perhaps it should be shortened to fifty years, science has found out that there is more to be learned about the physical world than can be ascertained by measuring and weighing, more than can be determined by the position of a pointer on a scale. Instruments are most valuable to science;

they are the tools with which it works. But they are not enough
for the thinking men of science today.

Certain prerequisites of the world we live in cannot be discovered by any physical means; only the indication that they
exist can be so determined. For this adventure of discovery
the men of science have turned to thought, pure thought. And
out of the constructs of thought they have created a greater
concept of the universe, an edifice of magnificence which corresponds to the physical world and at the same time appears to
correspond to a larger spiritual and mental world which must
exist back of the physical world. Why has the mind of man
been able to do this? Some say it is only because the mind of
man in some way partakes of the nature of the spiritual world,
for if it did not he could never even dimly recognize it, let
alone begin to understand it.

A New Unity

In man we seem to have that point where heaven and earth
meet, a place where the spiritual and the physical meet. The
intangible spiritual always becomes the tangible form. But in
man the spiritual retains its identity as spirit and mind, while
at the same time being tangible as physical body. Only in this
way would it be at all possible for what at first appears to be
small, insignificant, and limited man to comprehend in any way
or to any degree what is larger or greater than he is. That thing
which is greater than he is is also what he is. The part can never
encompass the whole, but the part could never recognize that
there was a whole unless it was of like nature. The mind of
man is beginning to recognize itself for the greater thing it
really is.

It is only as science has freed itself from the domination of
the pointer that it has been able to discover the greater universe. As man's thought has been able to soar, unconfined and
unrestricted, this new-found freedom of the world of the mind,

the world of thought, appears of increasing importance. In fact, of ultimate importance. The ultimate reality.

Today, Emerson would be well pleased. There would be no need for him to advise the relating of mental and physical law. They have been so related. Both are found to be aspects of a spiritual Reality existing behind all things; there is no division, but a complete unity. If mental and physical laws have the same source there must of necessity be a similarity, a reflection of their similar origin. Whether it be the mental or physical world we consider, we know that law does exist. There is cause and effect, and this action is definable and demonstrable.

But mostly we have been too involved, too concerned with the world about us and its operation, to pay much attention to the realm of the mind, the way it operates, and the laws relating to its operation. We seem to have studiously avoided consideration of it, when actually this should be our prime endeavor.

Powerful Emotions

Where may we look to discover for ourselves evidence of the action of some of the laws of mind which are a basic reality of the universe? We do not have to look far, just at ourselves or at a close friend. Two obvious things which we discover are love and hate. Their action in us and our reaction to them are powerful things. What occurs is specific and definite. Whenever one is a cause there is a corresponding effect. It operates according to law. Perhaps not a law that can be expressed in mathematical formulae such as gravitation or the flow of electrical current. But nonetheless exact and precise. We can explain the way it works even if we cannot express it in symbols.

As for love, when our minds are filled with thoughts of love for others it seems that we are surrounded by people and situations of a loving nature. Similar action holds true for hate. As our thoughts are occupied with hate we seem to be able to encounter nothing but hate in every aspect of our experience. And of course there are all the various degrees of love and hate which sometimes are too subtle for us even to be aware of. But some will say that of course we know all this, it is old stuff. Certainly it is, but when will the time come for each to recognize that love and hate operate according to law? This is important. Once we set a cause in motion we cannot avoid the effect. We cannot avoid the consequence of the thought of hate. But once that thought is changed to one of love we will have a new causative factor and accordingly experience a new result.

Ancient Wisdom Confirmed

Many years ago Plato made the axiomatic statement that if the head and body are to be in good condition we must first heal the mind and soul, that all the good or evil which befalls the body flows from them. Interesting for idle speculation. A nice bit of philosophy. But could it be that more than philosophy is involved? Could it be true, rather than just a bright idea? Perhaps more is at stake than just some fine moralizing. Our realization of this relationship of mind and body and our strict observance of and adherence to the principles of it, perhaps, is necessary rather than optional if the body is to be healthy.

It is just within recent years that the medical profession has confirmed the truth of Plato's bit of philosophy. Definite connections have been established between the nature of one's thoughts and emotions and the condition of the physical body. The mind-body relationship is no longer considered theoretical, but factual. Sometimes certain definite patterns of thought can be pinpointed as causing a specific ailment, and at times there is not always a specific bodily reaction but a general conditioning of the body for most any kind of ailment.

It is also possible that some time may elapse before science is able fully to confirm our further conviction that thought has a definite bearing on the nature of our experience in all *heal the soul, mind — the body follows.*

our affairs and contacts with others. But we do not need to wait for science to place its stamp of approval on this theory, we can prove it for ourselves, and are proving it every day.

When confronted with a psychosomatic condition, and most illness seems to rise from a mind-body relationship, the doctor *new medicine* seeks to correct the mental viewpoint and the nature of the emotional reaction so that the new basis of thinking and feeling may be constructive and help heal the body. From our viewpoint the same should be done to correct the bad state of our affairs so as to bring them around to a condition more to our liking.

Discovering New Evidence

There is a great Law of Life and aspects of It apply to every phase of our experience. Some of these we know. Of those we know, some we use to our benefit. Many more exist which we may not know or but little comprehend, and these we use to our detriment more often than for our good. But they are there, they are real, and to the extent we can ascertain them, to that extent we should endeavor to use them to the limit of our understanding of them. Experience alone will prove to us the validity of our concept of Law and verify our proper use of It. The time will come when we will discover for ourselves that the thought of hate can be just as damaging and painful as hitting our finger with a hammer.

As we look upon our lives, and perhaps find them in a rather chaotic or unhappy condition, we need to remember that here we have the evidence of Law at work. At the same time we know that such conditions can be changed through an inner action *changing the conditions of life* of thought. No, the mountain will probably not move for us, but we can know that we can control our thinking and our actions and reactions to life. And to a greater degree than most of us may realize we can bring about a healing, a harmony of all things in our experience through aligning our thought with the fundamental Reality of life, God. We can come to believe

aligning w/ reality God

that we are thinking centers in the one creative Mind and that according to the Law of Its nature our thought too is creative. And if we also come to believe that there is no "middleman" between ourselves and It, we are on the right track.

We cannot go to another for the creation of our new design for living. The ability to plan, to design, and to build is within ourselves. Every man will have to decide for himself whether what he is doing and thinking is constructive, life-giving, and contains the greatest good for himself and others. The proof of this is to be found in experience, evidenced in the design for living that has been created.

Freedom to Choose

The well-known philosopher Nikolai Berdyaev wrote: "God created man in His own image and likeness, i.e., made him a creator too, calling him to free spontaneous activity and not to formal obedience to His power. Free creativeness is the creature's answer to the great call of its Creator." This would seem to be valid in relation to physical and mental or spiritual law.

At all times we are freely creating the life we live. The ability consciously and specifically to better our lives depends on the degree to which we are able to believe in our basic concepts of the nature of Life with faith—a faith that rests on both intellectual and emotional conviction.

Everything in our lives is a creative activity of one form or another. Some people create good for themselves, others create bad, while most of us seem to create a little of both. But as we grow in knowledge and conviction, become familiar with the way law works, we are more and more able to swing the creative activity of our thought to the favorable side.

For centuries the comprehension and utilization of electricity were beyond man's power. When he finally reached the point of being able to direct its action to a certain degree, he discovered that it could heat and light his home, but that it could also deprive him of his life. Water may be considered in the same manner. It is necessary to life, but it also can cause a man to lose his life. These are two things which rightly used are of benefit, but whose action may be consciously or unconsciously directed to our detriment. A law does not care about the results of its action, it has no conscience, it knows only to act. It is impersonal. We are free to choose the direction of its action.

You Are Unique

The fact that law is completely impersonal does not mean that we are caught in a trap, caught in a whirl of senseless blind automatic activity. Nothing could be farther from the truth. Certainly law acts, but not until something moves it into action. This thing which instigates the action rests within our own personality and individuality, within our ability to think. And our ability to think arises from the fact that Life, conscious Intelligence, has become sharply individualized in and as us. This individualization does not mean that all people are rubber-stamp copies, or production-line products, but rather that each is a unique and individualized creation. No two blades of grass are alike, no two fingerprints, no two of anything are identical. This fact alone teaches us that it is the nature of Life forever and uniquely to individualize Itself in and through what It creates.

cause directed — not just random.

Two Great Realities

Even though Life does become uniquely individualized at every point of expression, the expression is always consistent with, and in conformity to, a basic unity that runs through all things. Fundamentally, we as individuals are never separated from That which created us. This leads us to the basic proposition that everyone has access to That which created him, direct access to the living Spirit which both is personal to him and at the same time surrounds him with universal Law which acts impersonally. These are the two great realities

No separation

of life—person and principle, Spirit and Law, or the Thing and the Way It works. There is a point of contact in our mind with the Infinite. At the center of our being in Spirit with which we may commune and from which we may receive a direct answer in accord with Law.

We cannot help but believe that God is personal to us, warm, colorful; and that from this Presence comes beauty, peace, and strength through silent communion. The true office of prayer is not so much to make things happen as to realize our relationship to the infinite Presence.

The eminent biologist Edmund W. Sinnott has felt himself forced to come to a somewhat similar conclusion as a result of his research into the nature of living things. He has written: "If God is what everywhere brings form and order out of randomness and finally molds dead matter into something that gives birth to spirit [in man], He can well be worshipped as Sovereign of the universe, of the lifeless as well as of the living. If man, however humble, shares this Universal Spirit, he should be able to make contact with it by that process of communion which through the ages has been known as prayer."

Each in His Own Way

Since no two persons are exactly alike, it would be presumptuous to tell anyone just how to approach the God he believes in. However everyone should be counseled to follow the gentle leadings that come to his own consciousness, for to him they must always be right. No one should feel that he has any cause to interfere with this most sacred of all human endeavors, the approach the individual makes to the God in whom he believes.

There are times in every man's life when he feels compelled to seek out his direct relationship to the Infinite. This would appear to be the action of the Infinite within man seeking to arouse and awake in him an awareness of what he is and his Source. There is something in the mind of man which is attracted, however subtly, to that which is like it—God.

The Law of Attraction

We are all familiar with such sayings as "Birds of a feather flock together," "Like attracts like," and "As you sow, so shall you reap." There seems to be something that brings together similar things. The mind of man seeks the Mind of God. There definitely seems to exist a Law of Attraction.

The more man seeks out the creative Power of the universe the more It seems to be attracted to him. The more he desires congenial friends the more he is surrounded by them. The more he seeks, in thought and action, health, success, or any other experience, the more are such experiences attracted into his life. The Law of Attraction, in other words, means that we attract into our experience conditions and situations corresponding to the nature and content of our thought. The action of the mind is like a magnet, drawing to itself all things of similar content. And this action is just as inexorable as that of an electromagnet, and there is nothing known that can block the magnetic field generated. The only thing that can stop it is for the flow of current to be switched off. Perhaps we need to switch off the action of some of our patterns of thought, and switch on others, so that what is being attracted to us is not all bad, not half bad and half good, but all good. We need to be selective in the types of thoughts we entertain in our minds, thus giving only good ideas the power of attracting their like in our experience.

We all stand at the gateway of our minds, at the master control board of our experience, at the drafting board of our design for living. Nobody else has access to them. On our shoulders rests the responsibility for actions resulting from the thoughts we entertain. And as our tomorrows become todays we will have irrefutable evidence of what we have attracted to ourselves through the very simple but definite truth of the axiom that "Like attracts like."

You Attract What You Think

In our use of the Law of Attraction we are not alone, unless we insist on trying to be alone. Mind made us free, and in that freedom we may turn to It for guidance. But nothing forces us to turn. If we turn in recognition of what It is and what we are, we may accept as a result of this direct relationship a new set of values, a stronger faith, a more complete sense of belonging to life, and an influx into our minds of a greater awareness of the true nature of the great creative Power that is the source of all things. And as we become imbued with an increased awareness of the greater good which is always available to us, we will find that we are attracting this greater good into our lives. The new complexion of our conscious thinking will reflect in new circumstances and situations which will have their source in the better and higher concept of our thought. The individual has every right to believe and to know that as a result of this new attitude his whole life will be changed, redesigned, into something better and more worthwhile.

Let there be no question in our minds about the Law of Attraction. If we look about us carefully we will see evidence of it on every hand, often in very simple ways. A group of people sits together, more or less unfriendly and chilly toward one another. Then a person full of friendship and geniality enters the group. What happens? He attracts to himself the previously unexpressed friendliness and geniality that is in each member of the group. What happens next? They all start to be friendly to each other. A crude example, perhaps, but a very obvious one.

Thought which dwells on pain or discomfort in one part of the body seems to attract similar conditions in many other parts which have no relationship to the original condition. A man gets into an argument with someone at the office the first thing in the morning. His mind is filled with argument. He encounters argument all the rest of the day; with clients, the waitress, his wife when he gets home, and the children. There seems to be no end to it, and according to the Law of Attraction there will be no end until he removes or switches off the type of thinking which is drawing into his experience that which is like itself.

The only way to become the kind of person we want to be, to live the kind of life we want to live, is first to be that person in our thought, live that life in our mind with unwavering conviction. The Law of Attraction will take care of the rest.

In using our thought, the function of our minds, we need always to remember that it is not our mind that we use. Rather, it is the individualization within us of the One Mind that we use, at the level of our awareness of It.

We are never alone, we are not isolated fragments of creation, but are part of one great Whole.

We may always turn to the greater Whole and accept more and more of Its good, abundance, and right action of which we may have been unknowingly depriving ourselves.

We attract to ourselves experiences corresponding to the nature of our thought.

8

LEARN TO THINK BIG

*We are potentially all things; our personality
is what we are able to realise of the infinite
wealth which our divine-human nature contains hidden in its depths.*

—W. R. INGE

WE APPEAR to measure out for ourselves carefully and assiduously the portion of life which we will experience. Figuratively we may use an eyedropper, a spoon, or a bucket with
which to do our measuring. Some people seem content to use
an eyedropper all the time. Others use an eyedropper for some
things and a bucket for others. It would appear that there is
no good reason why we should not use the larger container
at all times. No one or no thing ever specifies for us that we
must use a small container for some experiences of life, a large
container for others.

What is it that determines the nature and size of the container which we use to measure out life for ourselves? Our container has a specific shape and form, a pattern which is created
according to the nature of our faith and our mental equivalent—or the content of our thought.

And what is faith? Regardless of how exalted it may be, it
is only a definite way of thinking. Broadly speaking, faith
means a conviction about something that is stronger than

[handwritten: Faith = strong conviction.]

anything which may appear to deny it. We need a faith in the creative Intelligence in the universe, faith in the fact that things can be better, and faith in the spiritual Causation back of all things so that we are not confused by appearances. Faith is a transcendent principle, and through it we may overcome situations or change experiences more to our heart's desire.

However, no man can have this kind of faith in himself with the idea that he stands out separate and apart from the universe. He can have this kind of faith only, and in such degree, as he first realizes his unity with a Power greater than himself, *[handwritten: Unity w/ whole]* a Power in which he has the freedom to move about and to exercise self-choice, but at the same time a Power which will never change Its nature to suit the whims of his fancy.

This can well be illustrated by the law of gravitation. It is an impersonal law always tending to hold us in the position we take in it. If we wish to stand on our heads, it will hold us that way; if we wish to lie down it holds us in that position. But it will not float us around in the air if we choose to fling ourselves off a roof. We cannot change its fundamental nature. However, we do have freedom and volition within its nature. In this way we combine personal choice and impersonal law. *[handwritten: "Faith" in gravity?]* Our faith will not change the nature of this law, but because we do have faith in it we may relax in any valid position we take.

When we discover that we have a similar relationship to another kind of law which is related to our thinking, we shall at once have discovered the way to use the Power that is greater than we are, which reacts to us in accord with our faith in It.

The Need of Faith

This is the kind of faith that has been effective in all religious experiences. The faith that makes our thought creative of our good, the faith that makes prayer effective. This is the kind of faith that we should seek to entertain, that is real to our thought, feeling, and imagination.

We can count on water flowing downhill.

This faith some people seem to have naturally, a pure intuitive knowing. For others it comes through a development of some religious or spiritual conviction. In any case it should be our purpose to discover the law underlying such faith. And if we can come definitely to see that faith is really a certain mental attitude, why then should we not learn to acquire this attitude independent of any circumstance or situation and exercise it so completely that it will bring fulfillment into our lives?

To have faith in a Power greater than we are, faith in Its action as Law, faith in our ability to use It is not unique. It is possible to have the same faith in spiritual things that we have in things in the physical world. *Faith in laws we have discovered.* Every law that has yet been ascertained in the physical world implies a Power greater than that of the man who discovers it. And once a law is discovered, there is faith in the fact that it is law, impersonal and always consistent. And once this is known, man has faith in himself and his ability to use the law for his benefit.

Man discovered that water flows downhill. A Power greater than he is made the water. The action of it flowing downhill is according to law, it does not sometimes change and flow uphill, always downhill. If a water wheel, mill, or electric generator is placed in the path of its flow, man is able to direct the action of the law to his benefit. *Use the law we know.* In any endeavor, there is always the original creative factor, the accompanying action according to law, and the result. The result is according to the nature of our thought—the manner in which we have directed the action of the law—but the result will vary for each individual depending upon his faith in the nature of the creative Power.

Experience—the Measure of Faith

Everyday living would come to a quick stop if we did not have faith. There would be nothing that could be depended upon, there would be nothing that we could trust, we would

be fearful of our every move because of possible dire consequences. Every aspect of our daily living is based on faith, but
we seldom realize it. We have come to accept such declarations
of faith as commonplace and natural. We breathe, we eat, knowing that certain things will result. We turn on the lights, start
the car, light a fire, plant a garden without a bit of hesitancy,
fear, or doubt. We have faith. We know certain things work
in a certain way and that is all there is to it. This same kind
of faith we need to develop in another aspect of our living, the
most important aspect—the realm of the mind.

The caliber of our faith very definitely helps shape the container we use to measure out our portion of life. Another factor
helping to shape it is our mental equivalent. This presents some
very interesting ideas and possibilities. A little story will show
us what it means. Supposing a friend of ours, who is not too
well fixed financially, receives a wire that a long-forgotten relative has died and left him a small fortune. That at the end of a
year it will become his to spend and do with as he pleases. What
would happen to our friend? The odds are that he would suddenly become very happy, start to enjoy life, be in better health
than he ever was before, and generally speaking would be a
grand person. For him life would be wonderful. But remember
that all this would have occurred without his present bank
account being increased by even one cent; that would not happen for a year yet. In spite of this, right now he would develop the mental equivalent of being in possession of the in-
heritance and accordingly reap the benefits.

In some respects it would appear as though we were getting
the cart before the horse; that we were enjoying effects without
a cause. Not so. Once we are able to establish in our own minds
the mental equivalent of success, health, and happiness, success, health, and happiness become our experience according to
the Law of Mind in Action. When we are low in spirits, full
of aches and pains, and thoroughly miserable, if we would take
the time and trouble to establish in our pattern of thinking
the way we would feel if we were joyous, healthy, and happy,

that is what we become. We create in thought the equivalent of the way we would think and feel if everything were to our liking, and once that mental equivalent is firmly established there is no alternative but that through the creativity of thought such conditions are brought about. But this is not daydreaming or wishful thinking. The constructive creative power of such a mental equivalent, regardless of what it is the equivalent, rests in our faith in such creativeness, intellectual conviction of its effectiveness, and complete emotional acceptance. No doubts, no questionings, no apprehension as to whether it will or will not work.

Think Big

The question arises as to how big a mental equivalent or measure of acceptance we can establish for ourselves. Just a little bit of health, just a small degree of success, a pay check of a hundred instead of a thousand dollars? How big can we think? How much faith do we have in the creativeness of our thought? How much confidence do we have in the limitless nature of the Power that created us and the world? How much conviction that law will always function as law, not just sometimes? To the degree we can affirm such faith, confidence, and conviction, to that degree we can enlarge our mental equivalents and enjoy the tangible expression and experience of them.

In using the idea of mental equivalents for our new design for living, we first draw the complete plans for the structure of our experience, being certain that every aspect of the planning is correct and good, and then the structure that becomes built in our experience will be the equivalent of our plans. Too often we are prone to encounter the structure of our experience, then laboriously attempt to draw a plan of what it is like. This is like walking backwards. We bump into all manner of things, and wonder why we did. We need to turn around, face where we are going, and plan our next step. The fact that our foot may be in a mud puddle now need not concern us for we can step to higher ground. We need to do this rather than to sit down with our foot still in the puddle and bemoan our situation, carefully noting in our mind every step we took which led us to our predicament, and probably finding ourselves sinking deeper into the mire rather than getting out of it.

Remove Your Halo

We need to develop bigger and better equivalents of our future, what we desire it to be, and not continue mental equivalents of an undesirable past. So perhaps we need to get the cart ahead of the horse, perhaps we need to get behind ourselves and push a little bit, perhaps we have to remove our self-bestowed halo of conceit and know-it-allness and let our minds partake of their greater Source. We need to have a greater mental equivalent of what we are, and this means pulling ourselves up by our own bootstraps; but there is a Power within us which, if we let It, will help us to do it.

All this simmers down to the fact that the law of mental equivalents automatically responds to our thinking. Whatever we have an equivalent of in our total thought content will become our experience. This is only another way of saying that it is done unto us as we believe. We need to endeavor to learn how to believe and how to accept, to know that which we desire is *already* a reality. A reality in thought, in essence. But once it becomes a reality in thought, a spiritual reality, it automatically becomes a tangible reality. This process may take time and effort but it will gradually change our whole basis of thinking until, through the action of law, it will cause an equivalent of the thought to appear in our experience.

Measuring Life

Let us return to our idea of the container with which we measure out our portion of the good things in life. There appear to be two factors which determine its size and shape: faith,

1) faith

2) small or large?

and mental equivalents. We cannot avoid figuratively using a container of some kind. So let's make ourselves a good one. The material out of which the container is made may be considered faith. Is it strong or weak? Solid or porous? Can it be used for more than a few minutes without disintegrating? Be sure of the faith out of which the container is made. And the shape and size of the container may be thought of as our mental equivalents. We can take faith and form it into a small cup or a large bucket. In it we can put just a few, or many of the good things of life. Our mental equivalents determine the pattern and shape which our faith will assume.

We can experience life as something spacious and luxurious, or as something cramped and confined. The materials we use are the same, what counts is the way we use them. And don't forget there is no limit to the amount of material we can use. What are some prerequisites for richer living? Some ideas which may be simply expressed are: "I believe. I accept. I know there is a Power greater than I am. I know It is right where I am. I know It is working for me, as me, through me." If any doubts regarding these ideas arise from our past experiences, we may know that one type of thought will neutralize another, that a thought of faith will dissipate a thought of doubt, hope will replace fear, and love replace hate.

✓ We are always measuring out for ourselves the nature of our experience and the amount of it we will have.

✓ The container we use is constructed out of faith and takes the shape of our thought.

✓ We need to learn to have a stronger faith and to think in a bigger way, to have a more complete mental equivalent of the good we desire.

9
YOU ARE CREATIVE

For many things we can find substitutes, but there is not now, nor will there ever be, a substitute for creative thought.

—CRAWFORD H. GREENEWALT

THE UNIVERSE appears to be a continuous creative process. In trying to ascertain what started this process, we find that our search takes us back through the highly developed forms of plant and animal life, to lesser forms of life, to individual cells, to minute viruses which seem to show signs of life as well as a crystal formation, on back to individual atoms, which in turn resolve themselves into protons, neutrons and electrons, which are only concretions of pure energy.

At this point we find ourselves back at the beginning of any creative process. But what is involved? It would seem that there are only three things which are united in a larger unity. This entire relationship was nicely put by physicist Paul E. Sabine when he wrote: "The full realization of the free, conscious Self, the I that governs and controls under natural laws the atoms of the physical body . . . that realization comes only with the mystical yet wholly rational experience that God and the atoms and the human soul are *one* in essence, a spiritual trinity, three expressions of the living Soul of a living universe."

We find that there is only *one* thing from which all else emanates. Thought, Mind, Intelligence, an Infinite Thinker, God, Spirit—the name means little except for the *meaning* we give that name. The meaning we appear to have reached in our effort to establish the fundamental nature, the causative factor back of all things, is this: There is Mind, conscious and intelligent; Its word or thought takes tangible form according to the pattern of the thought and in conformity with Law, that same Intelligence acting mechanically and mathematically; and the substance which comprises the tangible form is but another aspect of Mind, energy.

The Way Things Work

Although we have previously expressed these same ideas they are again mentioned here because it is most important to get clearly in the mind the way things work. To state the whole idea very simply, all that we have just said means only this: Thoughts are things. The way in which thoughts become things is in accord with Law. We need not get involved in conjecture about the process or procedure between one and the other. If we can but realize the fact that there is a how and a way, even though we do not fully understand them, and understand that that which is seen comes from that which is not seen, then we will *know* thoughts are things.

So we find ourselves arriving at the self-evident proposition that in Its creative action Life makes things out of Itself by Itself becoming what It makes. If we cannot fully comprehend this, we can just accept it. Accept it in the same manner that we accept the fact that the creative action of Life makes a plant out of a seed, that It makes food and liquid into the bone and tissue of our body, whether we know or understand the action completely. In fact, no one fully understands the nature of the action or process, and probably never will, for it is the miracle and the wonder of Life.

No man will ever be able to delve into the heart of Life Itself, for to do so would be to become God, infinite Intelligence. We may be able to approach and become aware of the Creative Center, but to encompass It and fully comprehend It, never. It might be said that God could never explain God, God just *is*. So when we consider the nature of God we are thinking about something that just has to be accepted. We must accept the fact that there is such a Principle, that the universe is fundamentally a spiritual universe. Once we do this then our whole endeavor becomes the discovery of how to use this Principle in our lives.

And in this discovery we need always to remember that we are dealing with Reality, we are dealing with that which never began and which will never end, but which always exists. It follows as a matter of logic that all creation must of necessity proceed from, even while it remains in, this original Cause.

Continuous Creation

As a result we find that we are not living in a dead world, an isolated speck of life on a small pebble rocketing through endless space and time. We were not created and cast aside to be on our own to fare as best we might. Instead there is a living God, an active Mind and Intelligence, present in His own creation at all times and in all places and things. In other words, God is not only the creator, God is also what He creates; He is in His creation but not absorbed by it. God as conscious Intelligence is always thinking and His thought is always creative. It never ceases, never hesitates.

The whole concept of creativeness is simply and wonderfully demonstrated for us in everyday commonplace things and events which we accept without argument. What we take into our body makes the body and is the body, but we are always *more* than body and chemistry. The seed becomes the plant, the egg becomes the chicken. All through some mysterious process which we but dimly comprehend. We just accept this action of Life, avail ourselves of Its productivity.

The acceptance of principles is one of the basic things in every scientific research, and it also is one of the basic things in our inquiry into the nature of Life. We accept principles, for that is the way things are. There is no necessity to explain the *why* of a principle in order for us to avail ourselves of its action.

In our search for the source of the creativeness evidenced in the world about us, the principle we have discovered can be plainly stated: Not only in the beginning God, but all along the line God, and nothing but God, Life. Life is forever making things out of Itself through the simple act of seeing Itself as the thing It makes. But It must see through an interior vision, not an external one, as though It stood apart from Itself or creation. Would it then be too much to say that what God feels or thinks Himself to be, He is? We have probably encountered this idea many times, but not in just these words. "In the beginning was the Word, and the Word was with God, and the Word was God . . . All things were made by him; and without him was not any thing made that was made."

Your Place in Life

But where do we fit into this whole picture? What part do we play? Wherein can all this be of value in our outlook on life and in our experience?

Man is a part of Life, not apart from It. The life in man is part of the One Life. The mind of man is an individualization of the infinite Mind. The creativeness that is inherent in Mind is also in man to the degree man recognizes it. Life—God or Mind—is not present just in some places but not in others; It is not expressed partially at one point and fully at another. All of God is fully present at all times and in all places. Not just a little bit, although we may desire to recognize just a little bit. That is up to us. Just as it also is up to us to recognize, accept, and use the creative nature of our mind.

The whole relationship of man to Life, of man to his Maker, of our minds to the One Mind, has been clearly and concisely stated by great men of all religious faiths, by brilliant men of philosophy and science. God and Life are one. God and man are one. The creativeness of the mind of man is the creativeness of God in and as man.

In considering the creativeness of man and its relationship to Universal Creativity, physicist William F. G. Swann has said: "Viewing the universe as a whole, I cannot escape the fact that it is of intelligent design. By this I mean that the universe shows on a magnificent scale the same kind of inter-relationship of its working and efficiency of planning as an engineer strives to achieve in his smaller undertakings. It is not so much the failure to comprehend completely the universe which fills the man of science with awe, but rather the fact that in what he does understand he sees a plan akin to his own way of doing things, but one conceived with enormous clever-ness."

Emerson expressed it another way when he said that the ancient of days is in the latest invention. When we write a song or a play, create a new invention, or get any kind of a new idea, we are really carrying out the creative process of the Universe at the level of our individual lives. We all have access at all times to the same Mind, Intelligence, and creative Power that makes everything. God goes forth anew into crea-tion through each one of us in an individual way.

What Are You Creating?

In this idea resides the basis for all our creativity and in-spiration, all progress and expansion. And the use and applica-tion of the idea is so simple that it almost escapes our compre-hension.

All we need to do is to arrive at a mental and emotional conviction that there is a Divine Intelligence and that It is now operating through us; that because God knows, we also know; that the answer to every human problem is known in the Mind that knows no problems and is also known to us through our acknowledging that the Divine is flowing through us and the two are one. God continues His creative work through us, and in such degree as we accept this simple fact we experience more of it. On what other basis can many of man's greatest achievements be explained?

The Source of Inspiration

Great music: Beethoven would suddenly encounter in his mind a complete symphony. His only effort, and a somewhat strenuous one, was to hurriedly place it on paper while he could still retain it in his mind.

The experience of Einstein walking to a blackboard, a piece of chalk in hand, and writing a formula—a new formula that just came to mind. One he could not fully explain or verify. But one he said was true; one that had announced itself to him in such a way there was no room for doubt or uncertainty.

Even more recently there was the case of Dr. Edward Teller, the famous physicist who was working on the problem of developing a thermonuclear reaction, the basis of the hydrogen bomb. All others in their research and investigations were following similar paths which appeared would be productive. What happened? For some reason, impossible to explain, his thinking made a departure from all that was being done and he headed off in an entirely new direction. He solved the problem. Solved it in the only possible way it could have been solved. The previous path that was being followed was a blind alley.

Then there was the famous mathematician, Henri Poincaré, who lived at the start of this century and was concerned with the solving of complex problems, problems which others did not even have the courage to pose for themselves. In their solution he said that there is a time when the human mind seems to borrow least from the exterior world, and acts or appears to act only by itself. The mind alone, for him, seemed to become a creator. Then everything that occurred happened as though the mind were only an examiner interrogating ideas which were presented to it. In many respects in mathematical discovery the human mind seems to be a channel for something greater than itself. It accepts and announces the discovery. The discovery comes whole and complete.

The history of man is packed with countless similar illustrations, all of them fascinating. At times it seemed as though the impossible suddenly became possible. How can these things be explained? A stroke of genius, intuition, inspiration? Yes, probably all of these, but much, much more. All the ability involved in the logical process of reasoning could in no way enable the individual to arrive at the conclusion achieved. Something new entered the picture. Mind, infinite Mind, expressed Itself. Life went forth anew into creation. There is no other possible source or explanation for what occurred. In almost every instance such discoveries and creations as have flowed through and from the minds of men have been the result of sufficient intellectual courage to turn from the obvious, the appearance of things about them, from their own preconceived and static patterns of thinking, and encounter the pure unadulterated action of the creative activity of Mind. It is there if we but seek it out, recognize it, and accept it.

Your Wonderful Experience

In view of this, who can set any limit to the possibility of his advancement? Who would dare to set a limit on the expression of God through him? By what means, by what authority do we deprive ourselves of being that greater person we can be except through our own ignorance, our own blindness, our refusal to open our minds and eyes? Why do we insist on living within the limited confines of narrow thinking, thinking that refuses to recognize or make use of its innate creativity? The limitless productivity of the universe is within our reach, would we but take the trouble to reach. We need to wake up and look at things differently. We need to take a long look at life, and start to think differently about it. Life will always be life, but what it can mean to us depends upon what we think it can mean to us. Once we dare to stick our heads out of the cave of morbid, depressed and limited thinking we will find that a whole new world exists—the kind of world that we thought existed only in our fondest dreams. It is real and can become an actuality for us.

Since our lives are primarily mental, an activity of consciousness, it would naturally follow that we should come to believe that something wonderful, new and original, something continuously expansive, is happening to us at all times. On the other hand, how much of our time is spent in denying ourselves the privilege of entering into a greater degree of livingness? We are possibly bound by more negative ideas than we will ever realize. We keep saying, "I cannot. I don't know how. I lack the opportunity. Everything is against me." All of these statements are flat denials of Life Itself, and the creative flow of It through us. And what should be a constructive and expanding faith in accord with the creative nature of our thought becomes a limiting, contracting one. The result? We use the very power that should set us free to bind ourselves. Thought is a two-edged sword. It can be used to cut a pathway into a glorious future, or it can be used to cut down and sap every bit of life out of us. Perhaps nothing is good or bad in our experience except as thinking makes it so.

In this connection it is a very simple matter to reverse the entire process. The creative action is continuous. We but change our thought. Wonders can result if we can do this, if we can come to believe we are living in God and God is expressing Himself through us, and if we can apply this thought consciously to everything we do until at last it becomes an automatic action. Then we shall find ourselves on the road to a greater freedom, and happiness, and joy in living.

The creative Power of the universe is at a focal point in the conscious mind of man.

At the level of man, man is a co-creator with God.

The creative factor within man is ceaseless in its activity, which man cannot deny without denying the flow of Life Itself through him.

The creative ability that resides within man's thought may be used as he sees fit and he may design any kind of life that he desires to experience.

10 A NEW OUTLOOK

For (over and over again) there is nothing that is evil except because a man has not mastery over it; and there is no good thing that is not evil if it have mastery over a man; and there is no passion or power, or pleasure or pain, or created thing whatsoever, which is not ultimately for man and for his use—or which he need be afraid of, or ashamed at.

—EDWARD CARPENTER

THE MIND OF MAN has created many things, but none so cruel and so devastating as the concept that there is both good and bad in the universe. That there is God and the devil. That God grants some people fortune and success, and others He decrees shall be miserable and poor.

These ideas have bothered theologians and philosophers throughout the ages. But as we profess to be neither, they really need be of no concern to us. We are not interested in profound philosophical problems, nor in creeds, dogmas, or arbitrary dictates. Each one of us can know, or come to know, just as much about these fundamental propositions as anyone else living. Most alleged spiritual authority is merely an assumption which someone loudly proclaims and plausibly maintains, and when enough people come to believe in it, the subconscious reactions of their own thought seem to substantiate their claims until all become hypnotized. This kind of self-deception which leads to real conviction, right or wrong, is evidenced in an extreme manner by the number of "Napoleons" in padded cells in our mental institutions.

Rampant Imagination

If this seems like an unreasonable thought, we need only look about us and try to analyze the absurd claims, the illogical statements and unreasonable beliefs that people have about God, man, and the destiny of the human soul. In fact some seem to have inside information on the nature and horrors of hell. They are apparently people of wide experience and very well traveled, but as for us, we need to prepare no such itinerary for ourselves. In fact, even if we desired that there be a hell, who or what in a universe that is intelligent and harmonious could have created such a place? No, the only hell we will ever encounter is in our own minds, created by us for us by the nature of our own process of thought. But if it is heaven we desire, it is ours for the asking, ours for the thinking, today, right now, not at some future time. Heaven is what we make it, and we are making our share of it as we make the best of every moment.

Think Sensibly

Amidst and in spite of all the confusion of thought that surrounds us, let us try to maintain a rationality, being willing to accept anything that seems to be true, no matter from what source it may come, and at the same time maintain a balance of thought which can intelligently and without harsh criticism repudiate that which denies either the most profound logic of the mind or the deepest feeling of the heart.

It is impossible for the universe to be divided against itself. It is unthinkable that God, the Creator, would or could destroy His own creation. It is unbelievable that immortality could exist for some and not for others. On the other hand, it is not un-thinkable that since the very laws of life are neutral in their action, they must react to us in the way we use them.

The scientist of today has a great fund of knowledge about this world we live in. All this knowledge is predicated on the fact that the laws of the universe are consistent, reliable, and always work, from the atom to the island galaxy. Order is every-where manifest. The experiment book says that if we do a cer-tain thing in a certain way we will get a certain result. We always will. Nothing steps in and says "No." Or that "one time it will work this way, another time another way." No, law does not compete with itself nor rescind its action. God is never not God. Intelligent Mind is never not intelligent. It is only the way we use that Mind in us that at some times It appears to be inconsistent. This is the result of our ignorance or un-willingness to see things as they really are.

Life Is Not Against You

So it comes to pass that the very thing we fear most can come temporarily upon us. This would be but the result of the way we think. It would be our way, at the moment, of putting into use the principle that says it is done unto us *as* we believe. The entire situation resolves itself into the ques-tion: What *do* we believe? That Life can only be good? What It becomes for us in our experience can be either good or bad according to our belief.

But some will inquire: Doesn't God punish sinners? What about the bad in the world about us? As for the first question, if we logically follow through our line of thinking we see that there is nothing that can punish anything. The only effects that occur are the results of the action of law. If we seem to be in any way punished, or if another appears to be suffering for his sins, what is occurring is but a natural, normal consequence of the action of law. There is no displeased God hurling thun-derbolts of wrath at us, no malevolent spirit vying with God,

tempting us, scheming to stew us eternally in a kettle of boil
ing water.

This is a universe of law and order, a universe that does not
seek to destroy itself but ever seeks to create, to express the
harmonious nature that resides within it. But what of the bad
that we may say we see about us? Where does it come from,
and why? Still law at work. Directed either by individuals or
groups of individuals acting in unison. The fact that the
natural, normal forces of nature seem to be against us does not
mean they are bad. If a man builds his house on the flatland
adjacent to a river there is no reason for him to feel that the
river is bad when spring floodtime comes. He could very
easily have built his home elsewhere, removed from the river's
action.

The question also might arise about disease. Briefly answered, man's natural condition would have to be one of health,
otherwise he could never have existed throughout his long
history. There is something within man which ever fights to
maintain this health and ward off invasion of disease of any
kind. When disease does invade the body and secures a foot-
hold it is usually only because the body has been so conditioned
that it provides a fertile ground for the growth of disease.
What causes this conditioning? A great many medical men say
that thought does the conditioning.

So let us then turn aside from the idea that there is anything
in the universe we need to be afraid of, to the opposite viewpoint that ignorance is the only sin there is and enlightenment
the only salvation; that there is no sin but a mistake and no
punishment but a consequence; that the universe is just without
judgment; and that the laws of nature will favor us when we
work with them.

Accept What You Want

As for the life we are now living, there is nothing that de-
clares that this is the way it must be. Any experience of lack in

health, wealth, or happiness is not something that we must
suffer and endure as our particular lot in life. It is and will
be if we accept it as such, but we do not have to accept it.
Regardless of how bad things may be for us, how much we
might have felt in the past that they were prepared for us to
test us and try us, we know this is not the case. Life is joyous,
healthy, happy, and abundant. And it will become that for us
when we accept it as such.

We no doubt have had ample demonstration of the fact that
we have used the laws of life in a negative manner. Now we
are approaching the point where we are going to start using
them in a positive way for our greater good. It is just as easy
to use law one way as another. We can spend as much time and
effort designing what we don't want as what we do want. It is
a case of knowing what good we want and not deviating from
the idea or thought that will be creative of that good. No power
or force in the universe is going to look over our shoulder
and guide our hand, compelling us to design something other
than what we want. The idea that anything of this kind is ever
done can spring only from old negative patterns of thought
which we have not yet fully dismissed, but which can be done
away with.

The sincerest, deepest minds of the ages, without exception,
have all known that God is good and that the universe is not
divided against itself. They have all known that every man is
on the pathway of an endless destiny, forever expanding. They
have also understood that, temporarily at least, any of us can
obstruct the flow of Life Itself in and through us by the nature
of our thought.

The Hindu poet-philosopher and Nobel Prize winner Rabin-
dranath Tagore beautifully stated this idea in his autobio-
graphical writings. He said, ". . . one unfailing energy can be
seen. Its work is evident, but its form is not visible. . . . We
seldom give thought to this same innermost mystery that is
alive within us. Within me it has not always found an easy
path for its journey. It has met with obstacles at every turn.

... And yet, on the whole, I have known what the nature of His intention has been."

Your Only Battle

Man does not face an eternal struggle against some external force which desires his downfall. The only struggle, the only battle, the only thing that needs to be overcome is our own ignorance, our own lack of awareness and recognition of the beneficent Power and Creativity that is the source of all things. And we should never doubt the validity of our own considered judgment in such matters. There are no prophets other than the wise. Amidst the din and uproar of our lives, the accumulated fear, doubt, and confusion of the ages, there has always been and always will be a still small voice within each which evermore seeks to proclaim itself through us. Life has given us all we could ever desire. It is up to us to decide and discover for ourselves what the nature of Life is, and accept it.

And in our deciding what the nature of Life is we may accept the proclamations of the wise of the ages, the announcements of modern-day scientific research, or the dictates of the inner knowingness at the center of our being. They all say the same thing. We come to accept these proclamations, one or all, but not the morbid pronouncements that spring from a mind devoid of logic, blind to the nature of life, with thoughts immersed in fear, apprehension, anxiety, guilt, and hate. Let them alone! Let such live in the hell of their own creation. We are going to live! We are going to accept Life Itself in all Its beauty, joy, and goodness.

Beyond Appearances

For too long we have been discussing what it is we do not want, so let us turn our attention to how we can bring more of what we do want into our experience. But in so doing we need to remind and forewarn ourselves that we are not dealing with some system of thought or way of thinking whereby we may get something for nothing, or experience outward conditions which are entirely different from our inward states of consciousness. Life is from within out, and not from without in.

Regardless of how much conditions may seem to bear down upon us, how impregnable they may appear to be, how impossible it may seem to change them, we must always keep foremost in our minds that they are only effects—results of unseen causes and the action of Law. The starting point, then, for our experience of a greater freedom, a greater good, is the emancipation of our own thought. And as we start to free our thought we realize that in such degree as we work with the laws of Spirit, they will serve us. Even bondage itself, any sort of bondage, is but a false use we make of freedom.

The conditions about us are real, solid, tangible facts. We do not deny their reality. We acknowledge them all for what they appear to be to us. If we did not we would be putting blinders over our eyes, denying the validity of our senses, and refusing to accept the logical process of reasoning of our minds. The world is real enough. We face it, we don't need to avoid it or kid ourselves about it. We accept it for what it is. But we don't have to stop there. Most people do. And there they sit, with a sense of complete helplessness and of the fruitlessness of struggle. This we are not going to do any longer. We are beginning to know better. We know that there is a thought of some kind, an unseen spiritual cause, that is and must be behind every effect, every appearance, every condition, good or bad. The condition will change as the thought or cause is changed.

Don't Defeat Yourself

Even at this point, this will still be a new and startling idea of life for many. The reason for this is that we have become conditioned to the thought that we must struggle and endure,

Most destructive are ideas ← belief we need to be punished.

that we must be continuously defeated and everlastingly harassed. The only pressure, the only domination, the only defeat that can ever descend upon us from outward conditions can arise only as the result of some inward process of thought, the unseen cause.

The best thing any of us could ever do would be to gather together all the morbid, depressing, limiting ideas we have been carefully nurturing in our pattern of thinking and consume them in the fire of our newly established conviction and faith in the unity and goodness of Life. These ideas we will be getting rid of come from a feeling, conscious or unconscious, that we needed to be punished, which probably constitutes the greatest negation the human mind has ever entertained.

Security Is Within You

We start anew. We start with the proposition that Life is for us when we work with It; that we shall experience love when we become loving; that faith transcends fear, and peace will rout confusion, just as good will overcome bad. And in this process of the greater overcoming the lesser, there is no conflict, no struggle or battle. There is only the fact that as we work at the level of causation, that level which transcends appearances and conditions, the effects are not violently changed but harmoniously transmuted into something else, that something else being a fuller expression of God's good. And in considering this remember that if God's nature was not good the universe would be divided against itself and would destroy itself.

We now find ourselves in a position where we no longer need to let ourselves be buffeted about by conditions around us. Neither do we need to put on our battle uniforms and make valiant attempts to engage our enemy. Rather we take a nonresistant attitude toward our conditions. The battle we need to wage is an inward one. With our own thinking. We need to

don't resist the effects.

destroy not the appearance or condition but the old well-worn
pathway of negative thinking which was the causative factor.
We need not fight those things in our experience which bring
us insecurity; we need to recognize that the only security that
we can ever experience must of necessity arise from the security
that we feel within us. And that security within us rests entirely on our conviction and belief that there is a Power greater
than we are and that we can use It. We need a sound faith and
conviction in the nature of Life Itself, in Its essential good and
harmonious action.

Basically, all that we have to do is to learn to get rid of our
fears and doubts, to remove all confusion and bewilderment,
until at last we arrive, either through intuition or through the
due process of logical thinking, at a place where we can start
out with the simple proposition that "I am one with God, the
infinite creative Intelligence, and am no longer conditioned or
controlled by any external situation whatsoever." This is where
we start. This is the point of departure from being influenced
by conditions to influencing conditions. Instead of being in the
back seat of a runaway driverless car with endless hazards
ahead, we now find ourselves in the driver's seat, calm, cool,
deliberate; and with a knowledge of where we want to go and
how we are going to get there, we proceed carefully to guide
and direct our way along the highway of life.

The Source of Trouble

What are some of these conditions which cause us so much
trouble? Everyone will have his pet list. We all react differently
to any given situation. But here are a few illustrations of what
we are talking about: A famous doctor, with a heart condition,
said that he greatly resented the fact that his life was at the
mercy of anyone who could make him mad. In other words,
if he was not able to maintain a healthy normal reaction to
situations and conditions about him, his thoughts and emotions

would so increase the action of his heart that it could not stand the strain. In some respects this illustration is not quite along the line we have been talking about, but nevertheless it dramatically points out the relationship of external condition to thought and thought to bodily condition.

Another physician has said that the intestines act as a very sensitive barometer indicating the pressure that one's thought and emotions are under. They overwork or underwork and act *stress* up in all manner of strange ways with thought and emotion as the controlling factors.

And who is there who has not felt the effect of happiness or panic in a crowd? And regardless of how low one might feel, if he joins a party that is having a lot of fun he soon discovers that in spite of himself he is having a good time too. Then *fear* there is always the person with the best of intentions who suddenly finds himself caught up in the mob hysteria of fear or panic. In each instance the emotions, the mind, and the body of the individual react according to the conditions and situations in which he finds himself, unless or until he learns to live from within out, not from without in. But this does not mean that all external conditions should be barred from our experience. Far from it. There is too much to be enjoyed, too much beauty to be encountered, too much love to be experienced. We need to be selective in deciding what we desire to experience and through the creative nature of our thought make sure that there is more and more of that to experience.

Research in embryology and neurology gives evidence that the individual acts on his environment before he reacts to his environment. In other words, we in some way condition our environment before we react to it. Which is very much the same thing that we have been saying, that usually the conditions about us to which we react have in the first place been created and established by us through the process of the way we think.

A New Approach to Life

As we survey all the conditions surrounding us in our daily living we need to appraise them differently. First, they are not immovable and unchangeable. Second, we should not let them influence us to a greater extent than we desire to be influenced by them. At this point we can again remind ourselves that we should not judge by appearances, but should judge righteously. Look beyond the appearance and rightly determine the cause back of it, that cause which is unseen, on the mental and spiritual level. We need to believe in a Power greater than any negative experience of the world; a negative experience is only a misuse of this Power. In addition we need to walk calmly through life with a complete sense of security based on our certainty that our relationship to God cannot be disturbed by any external condition.

We design our new life from within, not from without. We turn to the creative center within us, to the creative power of our thought which is the action of Mind in us and as us, and at this point accept new ideas, building them into sound patterns of thought, knowing that the way in which they appear in our experience will make use of only the best possible materials consistent with the pattern for their construction. It might be wise if we do not try to do a remodeling job on our life. Oftentimes it is too complicated and costly. The design will get all messed up and we will find ourselves using too much secondhand material which is of no particular value, and more often than not completely useless. Start new, start fresh. We wipe our minds free of the influence of all undesirable conditions about us. Then we will find ourselves unhampered, unrestricted. We will be designing a new set of conditions about us.

This we need to believe we can do. But we also need to know that these things cannot happen unless our belief is soundly based on the nature of Reality, which we interpret as being the ultimate good that resides at the heart of Life, and then there must be compliance with Its laws.

We are in an eternal partnership of activity and creativity with Life—God.

Life established the partnership, but we have to become aware of it if all the conditions in our lives are to be filled with health, happiness, and abundance.

We need to let Life, God, be a co-designer with us of the new life we want to live, and when we do we will be surprised at the assistance that will be forthcoming.

11 YOU LIVE TODAY

No matter what looms ahead, if you can eat today, enjoy the sunlight today, mix good cheer with friends today, enjoy it and bless God for it. Do not look back on happiness— or dream of it in the future. You are only sure of today: do not let yourself be cheated out of it.

—HENRY WARD BEECHER

IN THE CONSIDERATION OF a new design for living it is only natural that we should encounter some rather deep and abstract truths, for we are dealing with ideas and concepts which lie at the very foundation of life. But we must always be careful to keep them at the simplest possible level and not get lost in a confusion of our own thought.

Of immediate importance to each of us is the fact that the universe in which we live is fundamentally a thing of consciousness—of volition and action—and law and order. And it is in such a universe that we must live one day at a time. But each day potentially contains all that any day can contain; each day can present us with new impulses, new inspiration, and new creativeness. God, the Infinite, can never become more than He is today, right now. All that Life is, is right now. All that Life has been, all that It can be for us is contained in the present

moment. We never have to wait for Life to become more so that
we can experience more. It is whole, complete, now.

We, each of us, could never have emerged from the universe
as conscious beings unless that Source from which we came,
and in which we now live, had the infinite elements and es-
sences of what we are. We do have a direct relationship with
the Spirit. And it is essential to remember that this is not a
relationship of our own choosing; it is not something that we
are evolving into, but rather that we are evolving from. Our
position is one in which we are becoming more and more aware
of something which existed before we were even conscious
of it.

Today Is Important

There will never be more of God, abundance, health, or
happiness than is available to us today. And the only time we
can experience what we may desire is today. We can't do it
yesterday, and tomorrow hasn't arrived. We have to encompass
right now in our thought all the good we can ever hope to experience. For out of that thought comes the joy of our life today
and the pattern for our experience tomorrow. But the present
moment can never provide us with more joy than we are able to
embody.

God is not removed from us by space or time, but is constant, immediate. However, the extent to which we become
consciously aware of our relationship with God is a personal
decision. We may postpone a greater awareness indefinitely, to
our loss. Life is declaring Itself in and through us this very
moment, urging us to wake up to what we really are.

Today is the most important day of our lives, it is the only
day we will ever know. We need to discard all theological concepts with their theories of a future heaven or hell. We need
to think simply and deeply and in accord with whatever the
real truth of the universe appears to be to us. Right now, God,

Mind, is complete, not divided against Itself. It did not create evil to combat. It did not create a yesterday or tomorrow in which to become more or less of Itself. It is eternal _now_. As we come to let our thought rest on this we find that goodness, love, beauty, truth, and order are immediately available, not far-removed in time. They are part and parcel of today, and we shall be more nearly right when we learn to include them in our day, not exclude them.

The Personal Universe

Our immediate relationship with Life, the Infinite, and all that It is, is so intimate, so personal, and so direct that it is closer to us than our neck vein, closer to us than breathing. We become cognizant of this relationship through an inner awareness, a feeling, an intuition. We all have this sense, but we do not use it sufficiently. But when we do, we find that God is not only where we are but is even what we are in our true natures. The knowledge of this and the seeking of an ever fuller awareness of it and fuller alignment with it means that we are always endeavoring to recognize ourselves as what we really are, the sons of God. We are now as much the son of God as we can ever become, and no moment in eternity is more important than the one in which we now live. If God ever had a creation, if God ever had a son, He has that son in each of us this day. He is begetting Himself in us now!

A greater inspiration, a fuller communion with the Infinite, and a more complete experience of the living Spirit, are all available to us. But they are only available to us _today_. There is no _mañana_ in Mind or Life.

The Past Is Gone

In considering the fact that we live today, we must admit that our todays become our yesterdays; they did exist, they were real, and not figments of our imagination. In our experience we are aware that today is really a continuation of yesterday, even as tomorrow will become a continuation of today. However, due to the fact that we are mentally more or less bound to yesterday and the past, through the faculty of memory, we find that we all tend to perpetuate the past into today and on into the future. It is in this way that we carry the mistakes of the past into the present. We persist in carrying the corpses of our undesirable past, which should be dead and buried, astride our back, and they relentlessly drive us down a pathway which can only lead to chaos.

Somehow or other, in some way or other, that time arrives when we realize that today need not necessarily be bound by the mistakes, the fears, or the failures of yesterday. In the past, we for the most part did what we thought was best for us at the time. But there is nothing sacred about those decisions, nothing that demands that they be preserved forever in our experience. If a time should come when we no longer expect more today than we experienced yesterday, we shall have limited the expression of the Divinity that resides at the center of our being.

How to Use Yesterday

We should use our past much in the same manner as science uses its past. In all of its investigations and research it brings to the present moment only as much of scientific thought as has been proved of value. Old ideas are changed to conform with new knowledge. Concepts and laws once thought to be inviolable are now in discard, being replaced with better interpretations of the universe. A lesser perception, seemingly important at the time, is always superseded by a greater perception. Wherein lies our ability to ascertain ultimate truth in any respect is difficult to say. But we must always allow ourselves to be open to the advent of it, just as science is continually

Don't relive the Past.

breaking precedents of the past to accept today's newest discoveries. In this lies our only hope of a future that is worthy of any consideration.

A complete reverence and worship of the past just because it is past, just because that is the way things once were, is an unwholesome situation. To the extent our minds dwell on and in the experience of the past we bar any new future. All too often we find this is the state of mind of many elderly people, and some not too elderly. In fact many feel that fifty is the dividing line. To reminisce is one thing, but to live only in memory is quite another. Whenever a person ceases to be creative, ceases to contribute creatively to life, then the great stupor sets in. The mind and the body start to stagnate. The mind turns in upon itself and the record of memory plays a monotonous tune. The vitality that fed the body ceases to flow and circulate freely, and every function and re-creative process slowly but surely starts to diminish, until a point of extinction is reached.

Such is the action of our past if we try to live it today. We cannot do it and live. The past was of value, it served its purpose. Properly approached, it can serve us wisely rather than burden us down. We want to know where our past pattern of thinking may have been wrong so that we do not repeat it. We can let the past teach us many lessons, but we must not let it dictate the nature of our future.

Don't Get in a Rut

For countless ages prior to the time that man cultivated the deserts, there was an endless monotonous repetition of seedtime and harvest. The cactus and sagebrush grew, put out their roots, distributed their seeds, and all this seemed to be an inexorable order of necessity. But when volition entered, when someone decided that it didn't have to be that way, the whole scene changed. The creative soil which had perpetuated a growth which was useless to the needs of man readily lent itself to a new purpose.

We find the same principle at work in our own mental and emotional life. We know from psychology and psychiatry that neurotic, morbid, and unhappy thought patterns tend to repeat themselves with monotonous regularity throughout life. The past maintains itself in the present. But since the past is gone, it can have no more creative power in the present than we give it. The old patterns of thought can be changed, and the same creative medium which sustained them will now sustain a new pattern and produce happiness. We need to be convinced that no matter what happened in the past, the future can be made of a new stuff. And this is not because of any change in the essence of Reality, or the laws of nature, but rather because we establish a new relationship to them.

We need to keep foremost in our minds that the laws of nature are never bound by precedent. For example, no matter what is growing in our garden we can uproot it, sow new seeds, and out of the same soil produce a different crop. Why then shouldn't this be equally true of our mental life? Of course it is true. But it is only a possibility until we actually do something about it.

Mental Laziness

This "doing something about it" is our problem. Certainly we want to live a better life, but will we go to the trouble to make a new design for it? Just how lazy are we? Really we are not as lazy mentally as we think we are, for we spend more mental time and effort producing what we don't want in our experience than ever would be necessary to produce what we do want. What is more exhausting than worry, more depleting than the mental and physical repercussions of fear, or more torturing than anxiety? No, we are not particularly lazy; in fact we are much, much too busy, doing the wrong things.

What we need is to have a complete reversal of our way of thinking; to develop a deep and abiding trust and faith in Life, infinite Mind, and to accept Its guidance which is ever available at the center of our being. In actual practice this would be equivalent to our saying that we are no longer conditioned by the mistakes of yesterday, nor do we any longer dwell on them. We resolutely put them aside and begin affirmatively to claim the good we desire.

The Time Is "Now"

The only time we will ever have is *now*, the immediate moment. The question that naturally arises, then, is how wisely are we using it? Are we retreating into the memory of the past, daydreaming into the future? We do not want to encumber this eternal moment of ours with vague dreams of tomorrow, nor clutter it up with refuse from the past. We can neither live in the past nor the future. But the thoughts of the past and the future can so color and contaminate our emotional and mental outlook that our reaction to this moment, each moment we have, will be a thing of despair rather than joy.

If we should have an unlimited mental acceptance of all good things for ourselves, is not this very act of acceptance a direction for the Law of Mind to produce more moments like this one? And would not such an acceptance have to be one that affirmed that we, right now, possess the desired good—not tomorrow, not the next day? For they never come. When there is such an acceptance of good, it must be on the basis of "believe that you have," *now*.

This does not mean that every moment of our lives will be filled with complete happiness, with everything that the heart can desire. However, we should learn to take from each moment only the joy, the lesson, the good that is in it. If we take only the bad, is it not out of this bad that the next moment will be born? Life is often filled with undesirable situations and conditions, and it can become a bed of roses only when we are willing to pick the thorns out of our flesh and throw them away.

Claim Your Good

In whatever aspect of living we desire a betterment—be it in respect to health, abundance, or happiness—we have to know that it is ours now. We establish the pattern now, we accept what it is now, we know it is our experience now. There is no difference between thought and thing. There is no time element in Mind, nor need there be in our mind. Whatever good we desire must be accepted as the present reality of our experience. Only *now* can it exist. This is but a simple hard fact: What we establish as a pattern of thought, what we believe in as real on the spiritual level of causation, is what becomes real in our experience. We must come to know that at the spiritual level of causation the physical manifestation of the cause as effect is immediate, is *co-existent with it.*

Regardless of how much we may say we believe in God, Spirit, or Mind, or in the creative power of our thought in the form of prayer, only by starting now, not tomorrow, will we ever come to believe more, to experience the proof of that which we do believe. We have in this moment the choice, the right, and the privilege either to maintain and support any pattern of thought we may have previously established, or to establish an entirely new pattern of action. We must decide, either to be as we have been, or to start to be what we desire to be. *Now* is the only time we can ever act.

Tomorrow Never Comes

We find evidence of the misuse and misunderstanding of the value of the present moment, of the creative nature of the *now*, everywhere we look: the person who is ill, bemoaning the fact that he is so sick today, but that perhaps tomorrow he will be better; the individual who finds himself in a state of poverty today and continually complains about it, but hopes that maybe tomorrow things will be better; or the one who finds no joy in living today but looks to tomorrow for some degree of happiness. How much are we pushing on as a future event that which we wish to experience? How many of us are prohibiting ourselves from ever experiencing that which we desire by refusing to accept right now, at the level of causation in our thoughts, what it is we desire? Possibly most of us, if not all.

It is often very difficult for us to realize that we are living in a timeless universe, and the fact that as far as the Infinite is concerned everything exists to It as a present reality, bound neither by the past nor by the future. Rather life is something that is eternally made new. "Behold, I make all things new."

It would be a good practice, indeed, if each morning we would say upon rising: "Something new and wonderful comes into my experience today. Today I bless everything I touch and am prospered in everything I do. Today nothing but love and good goes forth from me, therefore nothing else can possibly return. Today, this day, I am happy and whole." We need not worry about tomorrow. Tomorrow will take care of itself rightly if today is rightly lived. It is on the possibility of this fresh beginning that we must base our hope of the future todays.

Self-torture

We are all marked to a certain degree by the experiences of the past. And since we cannot, or should not wish to, obliterate memory, it becomes necessary for us often to reverse our thinking about the past. For instance, let us say that someone breaks a limb, suffers considerable pain, and goes through a long and trying period of recovery. It is most certain that there is no need of forgetting that he had gone through this experience; but at the same time there is no reason why he should continually relive the memory of the pain and anguish that went along with the experience. It is for this reason that psychology definitely states that it is not the experience through which we go, but rather our emotional reaction to it, which causes us harm. However, some seem to take a particular delight in inflicting such torture on themselves.

To remove the emotional content of undesirable experiences it is often of value to calmly and cooly bring them up in memory, to quietly live them over again and recognize them as events, but definitely realize that they no longer need have any content of fear, of horror, or pain. Remember the incident, but remove and dismiss any morbidity of emotion that surrounds it. It is a fact in experience, it was lived, but there is no necessity to keep on living it mentally and emotionally today. That was life at that time, but an entirely new life is being lived today, if we will but let ourselves live it.

Confess to Yourself

This is of course the secret of the confessional used by many churches, and the procedure often used by psychiatrists. It appears that the most effective form of confession is one in which the individual confesses to himself directly, clears up his own consciousness personally, and creates a new outlook on life by realizing that he has a personal relationship to the Infinite. We could even go so far as to say that this is a confession before God alone and to the self alone. It should be done without fear, without condemnation, and without judgment, but merely as one would straighten out the furniture in a room or revise or create a whole new procedure along any line of action.

We are able to do this in such degree as we know the Universe holds nothing against us, wishes only our good, desires only our success, and sees us only as It beholds Its own life manifesting Itself through our acts. And the time that we must realize that the Universe holds all this for us, that all this is available to us, that we may experience all this in our daily living, is *now*. There is no other time in which we may claim it or possess it.

The only time in which we may create or experience our new design for living is *now*.

It is never later than you think, there is only the fact that you may have barred from your experience of today much of the good it can hold.

The past has no hold on us other than that which we permit it to have.

We have to learn to live today, as this is the only time we will ever know.

We have to drain each moment dry of all the joy, happiness, and success it contains.

There will never be more of anything available to us than there is right now; we but need to accept it.

12
A LOOK
AT THE FUTURE

And life also belongs to God; for the actuality of thought is life, and God is that actuality; and God's self-dependent actuality is life most good and eternal. We say therefore that God is a living being, eternal, most good, so that life and duration continuous and eternal belong to God; for this is God.

—ARISTOTLE

For THE MOST PART man has always had a fear of the unknown. It does not matter whether the unknown is in the woods, around the corner, in the dark, or in a new city. If it is something that he does not know about there is a certain element of fear and uncertainty concerning it.

This seemingly innate apprehension evidences itself in many different ways. It even applies to any sort of change. Quite often a person will be content to remain in poor and undesirable circumstances because there is too much anxiety about making a change, even if the change is apparently for the better. To what degree it is instinctive, automatically a part of our makeup for the self-preservation of the individual and the race, and to what degree it is acquired as a part of our learning and educational process is hard to determine. Fear of the future, as a form of the unknown, is a big factor in most people's lives, but it should not be allowed to dominate and color every aspect of living, as it too often does.

From the viewpoint of the ideas we have so far encountered, we can see that any fear of what tomorrow may bring rests largely in what we fear today. In other words, since our thought is creative, since it is the mold of our experience, how could tomorrow hold anything that would be fearful to us? The only possible way for the future to become a thing to be feared is if we are creating that condition in our thinking today. The unexpected never happens, for in some way or other we can find the basis for it in the pattern of our thinking—actually we have expected it to happen. We rudely discover that the fearful experiences which we may be encountering could only have been born out of the turmoil and chaos of our morbidity of thought. Not too pleasant an idea to have to face, but nevertheless true. But the nice thing about this situation is that we can do something about it. We are not helpless. We can take a clear and definite position relative to the way we will think, create new patterns of thought free from all fear. To the extent we can live without fear today, to that extent will we be free of fearful experiences tomorrow.

We need to stop denying the nature of the Universe. It is good, harmonious. It is for us, not against us. It is not going to be to us tomorrow other than what It is to us today. If we have arrived at the point where we have complete confidence in Its perfect action, in Its ability to create, maintain, and sustain life within us today, to supply us with all our needs, then that is what It will do for us tomorrow, and tomorrow, and on into the future.

The Ultimate Future

Whether a person acknowledges it or not, any thought or consideration of the future in some way touches upon what he thinks or feels about his ultimate future. Expressed or unexpressed, ideas about immortality profoundly influence all our thought and action. To a large extent the views held in regard to immortality reveal what we consider the fundamental nature of Life Itself. This is always a very personal thing, and regardless of how much the individual may have read, how much he may have listened to the words of others, he will have to find within his own mind the answer that is satisfactory to him. Irrespective of what one may think about immortality, thinking will not make it so or not so, but the *way* one thinks about it will be reflected in the life he lives today.

On the basis of what we have ascertained to be the nature of the world we live in, and the nature of the spiritual Reality and Cause back of all things, what are we able to conclude about immortality?

The spiritual nature of the universe, God, Mind, Intelligence, from all viewpoints—science, philosophy, and religion— always was, always is, and always will be. Without beginning and without end. Eternal. Immortal. Timeless. If we are a creation of That which is eternal and immortal, if we are a creation of God and God is what we are, can what we are be other than immortal and eternal?

we are immortal.

What Is Immortal?

This does not mean that the body is immortal, or that any physical expression of infinite Intelligence is immortal, but rather that which caused the expression is immortal. The Divine source, the idea, the pattern is the immortal element. An idea in the Mind of God, Spirit, Mind, Intelligence, could not be other than immortal. The changeless is always giving birth to that which changes. We previously encountered the idea that our consciousness could not be other than the Mind of God in an individualized expression. Would it not be logical to assume that this is the immortal part of us? In fact could we possibly be other than immortal, since we are part of the Eternal? And to follow this line of thinking one step further, we have come to realize that it is the nature of Mind and In-

telligence always to be creative, always to seek expression, so is
it unreasonable to assume that there will always be some sort
of medium through which our mind must be able to create and
express? Where and how we do not know. But that there must
be a *where* and a *how* seems to be inescapable in a universe
which at its core is a spiritual Reality.

You Are Immortal Now

This brings us to a very interesting and profound idea. Right
now we are as much of this spiritual Reality as we ever will be,
although we will be continually becoming more aware of It.
If we are in any respect immortal we are immortal right now.
It is not something that may or may not happen later on. And
there is nothing that a man could ever do to earn it for himself or deprive himself of it. It is just the nature of things as
they are.

All the questioning, all the wondering, all the fearful concern
about our ultimate future will in no way affect it. The normal
and logical thing to do is to recognize and accept the idea that
we are living the Life eternal right now; that we are immortal
beings on the pathway of an endless destiny, one which is forever expanding. How futile would be the whole process of living if life were not eternal. We would be nothing but an idle
whimsy of an illogical God tossed into a chaos without meaning
or purpose. But nothing could be farther from the truth, as
we have discovered. Our birth was not just a mistake that will
fortunately be covered up in the grave.

A well-known scientist, William F. G. Swann, turned his attention to certain ideas of cosmology, the nature of the universe, and how man fitted into the picture. He stated, in effect,
that astronomy has determined that at some time in the far-
removed future, billions of years hence, our sun in all probability will disintegrate and the earth will no longer be able
to support life as we now know it. What of man? The spiritual
Reality which created the world, which created man, will

never cease to exist. Man as a spiritual entity will live on in a spiritual world, the reality of which science is just beginning to discover, but which religion and philosophy have long affirmed.

A Basic Belief

We cannot understand the true significance of immortality if we consider it for ourselves alone. Either it is a principle in nature or it has no reality whatsoever. And if it is a principle in nature, it is universal and applies everywhere. Not just some people are immortal, but all people. This may shock some and contradict certain theological dogmas, but if there is any truth in immortality, and there appears to be, then this is the way it would have to be.

The idea that God is not a God of the dead but of the living is both inspirational and logical; inspirational in that it is an insight into the nature of Reality, and logical in that it implies that that which is Life, the very essence and the very principle of Life, cannot conceive of death or nonexistence.

All peoples in all times have evidenced a belief in the continuation, the perpetuation of that essential element in man— Spirit. It appears to be something that he instinctively knows within himself; Life within him proclaiming Its nature. Many of the earliest traces of man that we have been able to discover are burial sites. Even before man developed to the point of being man as we know him today, he buried his dead and placed beside him artifacts for his use in a future life.

In the not too far removed past any idea of immortality was considered by many to be wishful thinking, a forlorn hope, without a basis in fact or reason. But not today. The Spiritual Universe is a firm and necessary reality, and we, at the center of our being, are spiritual entities and part and parcel of a timeless, eternal Reality—infinite Consciousness and Intelligence.

The Great Goal

A great burden of fear will be lifted from us when we come into the realization that the future of all humanity is a certainty, according to the very nature of the Power that is greater than we are. All share equally in an eternal existence. We are all incarnations of God, God is what we are. God is not lost, neither can we ever be. We never need to prepare to meet our God, we are meeting Him every day. But what we do need to do, and what we will always be doing, is to express more and more of His nature through ourselves. This is the endless pathway. This is the immortal and eternal endeavor, the continual upward spiraling of our awareness of God as what we are. We may do it slowly, or rapidly; we may delay it, or we may hasten it. A greater knowledge, experience, and expression of God is always our goal, which may and must be ever more fully attained. Life is. It will never be more eternal than It is right now. The expressions of It may change, but It can never change.

We all are facing the ultimate future today if we but realize it. And the possible reward or punishment of any individual life is not for another to determine, for we are all punished or rewarded according to our own acts. Every man must of necessity be a law unto himself under the one great Law governing all things. The same goal lies ahead of every man. How difficult he makes his climb, how much he hinders himself, is up to each individually. No one can act destructively or chaotically without suffering a logical result, but at some time along the pathway of experience we will learn to follow a line of thought and endeavor more in accord with the nature of Reality which will produce only good. In the meantime we need to remove all condemnation and judgment from our thought, for we realize that every man is on his own pathway and everyone will arrive.

Things to Come

Such a concept of immortality can bring about a vast change in our consciousness. For while we neither condone nor praise our own mistakes or those of others, we see that there is a flexibility in nature, that everything is in a process of growth and evolution toward the greater possibility, and that even the pain or suffering of our mistakes will cease when our lives are reordered to conform more nearly to the eternal Divine nature and pattern which already exist within us and within all things.

The ultimate future? Its place in our thought and action today? Immortality is not some Divine far-off event but is an ever-present reality. We can never experience it more than we permit ourselves to experience today. We can't wait for it, we now have it. The ability to experience spiritual Reality can be acquired only now, never later. By the same token the future, immediate or ultimate, is being born in us today. What it holds, what it means to us, is up to us, in the way we think and the way we act.

The nature of things to come is based on the design for living we establish today. We have to be certain that the new design is founded on the best we know, the best we can imagine, and in the closest possible conformity with our inner awareness of the nature of God. Then will our fears be allayed. Then will we be able to live today and each day with that joy and happiness that flows from the Eternal, which is good and knows no otherness.

Today we should accept all of Life, not just a part. Accept it without fear, without fear of the past, the present, or the future. There is always today, this glorious moment to experience more of what we are—God in us, as us.

In no respect need we be concerned about the future; we may determine for ourselves what it will be.

Life is not against us and our tomorrows can be good only if we align ourselves with Its nature.

Immortality is a principle inherent in the Universe; no one earns it and no one can deprive himself of it.

Everyone is on the same road leading to the same endless destiny.

Each is as immortal now as he ever can be, and to live up to the full meaning of this concept is the ever-present challenge.

13

SUCCESSFUL LIVING

> *We need only in cold blood act as if the thing in question were real, and it will infallibly end by growing into such a connection with our life that it will become real. It will become so knit with habit and emotion that our interests in it will be those which characterize belief.*
>
> —WILLIAM JAMES

ONE OF THE MOST DIFFICULT THINGS for anyone to realize is that he is always a success! As contradictory as this may seem it is nevertheless true. We are always being successful, we are always achieving the goal we have set up for ourselves in thought. Some people may win themselves terrific success at always being a failure in business. Others may succeed in always experiencing ill-health. Still others always succeed in being friendless. We always succeed, so our immediate problem is not one of success, but what *kind* of success we are having.

We need not worry or wonder if we will succeed, but instead we need to direct our attention to that in which we really desire to succeed. We find ourselves right back at the starting point, the only starting point—thought. What are we thinking? What is our habitual thought pattern? What is our total thought content? Here is the beginning and the end, the cause and the effect.

Most of the time we have been too successful in the wrong things. What we now desire to do is to succeed in having a greater experience of good. Where do we start? What is the best procedure to follow? We start right where we are and with what we are. There is nothing to wait for, no more opportune time, and no other place to start than right where we are. We start with what we are thinking right now. As for procedure, this is up to each individual. No one can tell another how or what to think, but certain suggestions can be made as to advantageous ways to think.

Planning Your Success

In our desire to start to succeed in a different way than we have in the past we create a new balance in our pattern of thinking, establish a balance that is more favorable toward good. By establishing in our minds ideas declaring that a greater good now exists in all aspects of our living, by consciously believing and accepting this as reality, we begin to build up new patterns of thought. We make such statements only when we know they are in conformity with the highest good for ourselves and for others. We know that the statements we make concerning our good are spiritual realities. Our pattern of thought is complete and now existent as a spiritual entity. Its appearance as an actuality in experience automatically follows.

We build up, idea by idea, thought by thought, concept by concept, the good we desire. As we do this the negative content of our conscious mind and subconscious mind will be replaced, then we will have a new pattern, a new design for living, through which the creativeness of Life will flow anew into our experience.

The mold of our experience is a pattern of thought. The design for the life we live resides in the mental plans we have drawn. The pattern is changed little by little, item by item, until the old is replaced by the new. We usually find many of the old unwanted aspects are stubborn and hard to remove, but we conscientiously proceed to plant new ones whose growth will soon overcome all unlike them.

We have to be consistent in our designing. Even as difficult as this may at first appear to be, each positive constructive thought that replaces a previous negative one builds up a swelling tide of affirmation and conviction that of necessity will some day tilt the balance so that a greater abundance of good will flow into our experience.

Be Consistent

Without realizing it we too often negate what we affirm. Take the situation of a man who owned a store and sincerely prayed, morning and night, that his business would prosper. At these times he believed and accepted without a question of doubt. But then what did he do at the store all day? All he could see were the countless people who walked past without coming in. Even those who did come in he more or less overlooked. All he could think about were the people who were not coming in! So they didn't come in, regardless of his prayers. His every thought was some form of creative prayer. He never took the trouble to see how his thoughts added up at the end of the day. But they were on the negative side and so was the business at the store. Consistency is all important. Consistent negative thought gets us into most of our trouble; consistent positive thought is the only thing that can get us out.

We must not lose sight of the fact that what we are talking about has nothing to do with will power. We are not forcing anything to happen. We do not coerce God. We cooperate. As we recognize God's universal nature as good, as the source of all abundance, and as the perfection that resides behind all life, then we may come to accept all these things. We do not create them of ourselves. We accept them, and in our acceptance of them they are manifested in and as our experience.

On this basis it would appear that our experience of any

degree of poverty, sickness, or unhappiness is but a successful manifestation of our negative thinking, a perfect demonstration of the Law of Mind in Action. On the other hand, abundance, health, happiness flow to us and through us as we accept them from their infinite Source. We may create our own hells, but we can only accept heaven from That which is heaven. As we create an unlimited acceptance of the good life for ourselves, in spite of all appearances to the contrary, that is what we will succeed in living.

Even though we may only be able to accept a little of our better life at first, each additional successful experience will breed more of it. Success breeds success, so let us be sure of the direction in which we are going.

Avoid Civil War

Although we are a whole individual we have several distinct aspects. We have been speaking primarily of thought, and our acceptance in thought of the greater good we desire. But we also have our emotional nature, and we live a life that is filled with action. Thought, emotion, and action must be unified in purpose and intent. There must be no conflict between them or we will find ourselves in a position where one will negate the good in the others. We must intellectually accept the truth of our affirmations of good; we must emotionally embody and feel them, live them right now; and our every act must demonstrate that we know they are actualities. It makes no difference if they are on the spiritual level at the present moment, they have to be there first in order ever to be anyplace else.

So we must hold ourselves together and not try to go in three directions at once, or let ourselves become involved in a civil war. What we are expresses itself as thought, emotion, and action. Their Source is one; keep them unified in It, and guided by It. Maintain a balance of power between them, don't let one run rampant over the others. Cooperative effort between them will enable us to successfully experience a richer life.

The Foundation of Success

All truly successful people carry with them an atmosphere of affirmative expectation. They expect to prosper and succeed. Almost automatically situations and conditions surround and are attracted to them that make success possible. It would be impossible for them not to be successful. Some people just naturally think success; others of us seem to labor with the idea. In such a case we must re-educate ourselves and the way we think. The end result of such a process is that we arrive at the point where we come to know that we are daily guided and governed by a supreme Intelligence, and acted upon by a Power greater than we are. Right here is where faith plays its very important role—a faith that is simple and that we already possess.

We never try to argue ourselves into believing that we are alive, or that the world is round, or that water is wet. We accept these simple propositions because something within us knows that they are true. We also accept more profound conclusions with equal faith. Man is born to believe, to have faith in something greater than he is, for he is a Divine being and always carries with him some echo of that infinite Source in which he lives and moves.

This faith that we should have is not a faith in some extraordinary belief, in something we just hope is true, but rather a fundamental conviction that every normal person should hold about life, whether he has ever analyzed it or not. A faith in an overshadowing Presence which guides and a Law which reacts. This faith is in perfect keeping with the best that man has learned about himself and the world he lives in.

And on such a faith, such a foundation of security, rests all conscious seeking of successful attainment of the better life.

Such a faith designates the Source of the greater good and the way in which it becomes our experience.

We always succeed.

We need to learn to succeed in the right things.

This we can do by declaring and affirming the good we desire, and having a firm belief and conviction that it is ours right now.

What we believe in is firmly established as a spiritual entity and as such must of necessity manifest itself in our experience.

We actually create nothing, but only accept the abundance we desire from the infinite Source of all abundance.

14
THE ABUNDANT UNIVERSE

> *He contributes to the consciousness of God*
> *who discovers truth, creates beauty, adds new*
> *treasures to the psychic possessions of mankind*
> *which are its only permanent possessions. The*
> *recognition of God . . . with the cosmic drive*
> *of which the life-personality is the spearhead,*
> *is the only road to individual self-fulfillment.*
> —LOUIS BERMAN

I T IS HUMAN NATURE to desire an abundance of all things. We desire a lot of happiness and joy. We like to be surrounded by beauty and friends. We want to have all our needs supplied, and the luxuries too. We want to love and to be loved. We like to experience success and health. In other words, we want to have a richer experience of all the good that life has to offer.

The question that presents itself to us is whether or not there is in the nature of the Universe anything that prescribes that we shall be able to experience just so much abundance. Or whether, if we possess an abundance in some respects, are we depriving ourselves of abundance in others?

As we look about us we encounter no evidence that nature in any way is other than abundant: the grains of sand on the beaches, the countless stars in the heavens, the blades of grass, the leaves of the trees, the myriad forms of life, all are signs that point to a limitless creativity and productivity.

All that exists in the tangible world flows from the invisible world of the Spirit. Nothing can limit God, and God does not limit Himself. So when we speak of abundance are we not speaking of the abundance that the Infinite encompasses and is? It is all there. As much abundance as we can conceive of cannot even begin to include the whole, but the amount we can conceive of is what we will have.

There Is More than Enough

We need to expand our thinking of what abundance means to us. As a first step let us learn a lesson from the scientists. They discover and use the laws in nature. They are not afraid that these laws will ever wear out or become depleted. They use them with perfect confidence that they are available for limitless use. In much the same way we may add two and two and get the sum of four. It does not matter how seldom or how frequently we add two and two, the result will always be the same. There is nothing that determines that we may use the laws of addition so much and no more.

Too often we seem to have the feeling that Life is of just a certain size, that It can only mean so much to us. That just a certain amount of It is measured out for us to experience: if we have abundant success there is not enough abundance left for us to also have health; if we love our immediate family there is not enough love left to have a sense of love for all our fellow men; if we have two friends that is all the friendship we can express; we can get along with some people but not all people; we can be happy and joyous for only an hour or two a day.

The laws of nature are limitless, whether they be mental or physical. But just as we have limited ourselves in the use of physical law in the past by ignorance of its nature and the way to use it, so, are we not limiting ourselves in the conscious use of spiritual law?

We have to realize that law is always available, always ready for our constructive use. And that what determines the degree to which we use the law is the nature of our own thought—the directive factor, the pattern through which Life flows, the mold in which Life becomes manifest. We have to carefully watch what thoughts we hold up to the mirror of Life that will be reflected back to us in our experience. Is our pattern of thought one of abundance or limitation?

Grow Up Mentally

Life is ever ready and willing to become to us what we think It is. It will be a lot or a little. Rich or poor. Happy or sad. Abundant or scanty. We do the choosing and we live with our choice. The choosing is done by what we think and the way we think; not just sometimes, but all the time. Always remember that regardless of the way we may have chosen in the past we are free to choose anew. We may enlarge our thinking as to what Life is and how much of It we are going to accept.

It would appear that as a person gets older the abundant universe seems to get smaller. The child matures into the adult, but does he carry with him the childlike faith he had in his world of supply, or does he lose it? The child in the protective shelter of the home and the love of his parents has complete faith and conviction that all his needs will be taken care of. But the child's world expands with the entry into school, then come the uncertainties and conflicts of adolescence, followed by the departure from the home and the entry into the business world and the national life. He finds himself becoming more lonely and somewhat lost in an expanding universe. Often he loses the faith, the trust, the security he had in the arms of his parents. At this point man seems to stand singularly alone, a point he has reached by gradual steps. There seems to be but himself and

God. And if he but knew it, that was all there ever was. The love that embraced him as a child was the love that flowed from God. The abundance that the universe had for him then is still available from the same source—God. Nothing has changed; that is, nothing of Reality has changed. But he has gradually limited the degree of his experience of the abundant universe.

Let Life Expand

It is at this time that the individual must keep his eye single, must see beyond all appearances. He must turn within and discover that he is all that he ever was, that at the center of his being there is the Presence of God in him, as him. This is all he has ever been and ever can be. He needs to establish in his relationship with God the same childlike faith he had in his parents. Life in all its fullness, in all Its limitless abundance of all good things, is still there awaiting acceptance.

Where we may in the past have accepted but a little of the abundance of Life, we may through a reversal of our thought, reverse not the action of the Law, but the way we are using It. Through the nature of our pattern of thinking, where we may have used the Law to measure out limited amounts of abundance, we may now use It to measure out as much as our thought can encompass.

Practical Procedures

In actual practice we may find that in thought we wish to deny every sign or evidence of lack and then follow up such a denial with an affirmation of its opposite. The denial will have much the same effect as erasing figures on a blackboard, and the affirmation will have the effect of setting down new figures. In erasing the old figures and writing new ones there is no forcing of anything. Rather it is only a new decision that we make, and with a good-natured flexibility we continue to re-assert it until the seedtime of our faith and conviction matures into a harvest of fulfillment in our experience.

Naturally all this calls for a deep and abiding trust, a complete conviction, and an equally great patience with one's self, for after all we are human beings subject to surprise and disappointment, to over-optimism, and sometimes to deep depression. But through it all, if we maintain a calm and persistent attitude of gentle affirmation, the very pressure of this affirmation will gradually dissipate and reverse the negative thoughts and will redirect our lives—will so remold and re-create all the conditions and experiences surrounding us that finally we see with complete conviction that we are on the right track.

And we are on the right track when we know that our abundance does not depend upon the things or people about us. Abundance in our experience resolves itself down to the simple basic fact that it is a matter of what we think our relationship to God is, and the persistent pattern of thinking we establish for ourselves.

The important thing right now is to know that we are headed in the right direction. Are our thoughts a little more constructive and more expectant of good than they were yesterday? Can we see that Life holds more abundance for us than we have yet accepted? And can we accept that more? Are we able today to maintain even a slightly more affirmative attitude than we have previously? If we are doing this progressively we are certain to have an increasingly fuller experience of the limitless abundance of good that is ever available to us.

The Universe holds an abundance of all good things.

What It may become to us is determined by what we think It is.

We must let our thoughts encompass more and more of what we want and at the same time become more of what we *really* are.

Increased abundance of every good thing is always the greater possibility and becomes an actuality only as we accept it.

15
THE POWER
OF LOVE

Love not only cures and revitalizes the individual's mind and organism; it proves itself to be the decisive factor of vital, mental, moral, and social well-being and growth of an individual.

—PITIRIM A. SOROKIN

Probably no other word in our language has been so misused and misunderstood as the word love. In fact it is used so often, in so many different ways, that it is almost impossible to give it a clear and concise meaning in spite of the dictionary definition. We say we love our family, love our children, love our country, love a painting or a motion picture, love a steak, flower, or song. Perhaps all we are trying to say in many cases is that we have a liking for this, that, or the other thing. If so, then where does love come in, that love which has been referred to as the most powerful thing in the world? Just what is it?

In order to clarify the situation a little, we might start out with an idea advanced by anthropologist Ashley Montagu, who feels that the one word which more nearly indicates what love really is, is *interdependence*. On this basis love would appear to be evidenced in every aspect of existence. It would mean that love is manifest on the inorganic level as well as the organic level. The interdependence of one part of the atom on another, the interdependence of one cell on another, of one organ on another. And in such interdependence there is always a reciprocity. There is a giving and a receiving. Love is not a one-way road but a harmonious comingling of the parts.

Illustrative of this idea is the story of the man who was taken on a tour of hell and heaven. In hell he saw people seated at long tables ladened with food, but they were thin, hungry, and emaciated. They had a long spoon tied to each arm—such long spoons that they were unable to feed themselves. When heaven was visited he also found people seated at long tables ladened with food. They too had a long spoon tied to each arm, but everyone was well fed and happy. They fed each other!

It would seem to be a fundamental fact that love is the basic reality of life. This would in turn give rise to a firm conviction that God is love. God, creative Intelligence, depends on His creation for expression, the expression depending on God for its existence. God could never stop creating or loving, neither can the creation cease loving or expressing God without limiting its experience of the Source of its existence, in which case it would gradually cease to be. In the mind of man we find the only created thing which can consciously deprive itself of accepting God's love, and when this is done the results are disastrous. Note that we said *deprive*. God's love for man is always there, whether man cares to recognize it or not.

Is Love Practical?

There has been much written and much sermonized on the theoretical aspects of love, but what about its place in everyday living? Is there anything practical about it? One thing that comes very close to home for all of us is the state of our health. Does love mean anything in this respect? Probably more than any of us cares to admit. When there ceases to be a feeling of interdependence with another, a feeling of love, this is usually replaced with hate. Love attracts, hate repels. Love attracts good, hate repels good. Love attracts health, hate repels health. Hate and its associated emotions cause the body to malfunction; there is a lack of harmonious action and interdependence of the parts. The rhythmic action of the heart is disturbed, the gastrointestinal tract refuses to function properly, and often the gastric juices start eating into the lining of the stomach which contains them. The fluid secretions of the gall bladder concentrate into small stones. The joints become as stiff and inflexible as the pattern of thought.

What happens next? We start to hate our body for the way it is acting. We hate the condition of our heart, our stomach and our innards in general. This aggravates the situation even more. The list of things that hate, the lack of love, can do to the body seems limitless. Not that a certain ailment always may be caused by a certain type of thought, but medicine today more and more correlates the two. And the most frequent culprit in the realm of thought and emotion is the lack of love and the cultivation of hate. It would appear that as a matter of necessity for our own well-being we cannot afford not to love everybody and everything. If this would seem to be too big an order, then at least we must not hate. Forgetting everything else, we are faced with a simple matter of expediency, of expressing love for our own preservation. The physical state of health we can enjoy depends to a large degree on the amount of love or hate in our thought.

Find Something to Like

Just as there is a harmonious reciprocal action of love between the Infinite and Its creation, between love in the thought of man and his body, so there is also the reciprocal action between the expression of love on the part of a man for the conditions, situations, and people in his experience. No condition or relationship can be changed for the better by hating. Hate only aggravates, makes things worse. If things are not to our liking there is no need to hate them or fight them. This uses up a lot of time and energy, makes us ill, and we get no place unless it is a matter of getting where we don't want to go.

The only solution, our only healthy, normal, creative avenue of approach is to let the reciprocal action of that love inherent in the Universe flow in and through us and out into every phase of our experience. If it flows out, it has to return. Regardless of the situations, the conditions, or persons that we may feel inclined to dislike or hate, we must resist the inclination. In some way we have to find something of value in them, no matter how big or little it may be. Find something to like. Then concentrate on that and that alone, ignoring all the things we dislike. Once this is done then there can start to flow forth from us a feeling of love. And once the flow is started there is opened up the channel of reciprocal action. As we give, so will we receive.

The action of love in and through us must be universal in all of our experience. We cannot love in one direction and hate in another. Once we cut ourselves off from the beneficial action of love in any respect we cut ourselves off in every respect. We cannot survive by liking the Joneses that live to the east of us and not the Browns to the west. We have to include both. This does not mean that everyone has to be very intimate and chummy, but that we cannot afford to have dislike and hatred gnawing at our minds and bodies. It is just plain common sense.

You Can't Live Alone

It is very likely that one of the greatest problems facing the individual and the world as a whole today finds its roots in a lack of love, a lack of a sense of interdependence. Everything is part of one great harmonious whole. Once this balance is upset, once there creeps in a feeling of complete independence, then trouble starts to appear. The family unit needs to have a feeling of love permeating it, a sense of interdependence. Husband, wife, and child are bound together by a feeling of love for each other, a dependence of one on the other. This does not mean that a child should not grow up, mature, and go out into the world; but it does mean that no one can become so self-centered, so self-sufficient, that he can cut himself off from any other person by a feeling of dislike or hate. It could be that the same pattern of action holds true on the international level. Something to conjure with.

The Need to Love

Where else may we find examples of the need and necessity of love? Children, normal and healthy at birth, who by circumstances are relegated to an orphan's home where love is lacking, soon become emaciated and sickly. The death toll is heavy. There is a lack of an expression of love that cannot even be consciously appreciated. No fault on the part of those whose responsibility it is to take care of these babies, but time and the press of duties in the institution may not permit the full expression of love that is needed. Kittens? Yes, they respond too. Any kitten that is petted and loved is said to grow faster and be happier. What about the person with a "green thumb"? The answer is probably very simple. He loves the plants he is working with. Luther Burbank did. He loved his plants and talked to them. How they grew and produced for him! And from his time on man will continue to benefit from his expression of love for his plants.

It would be difficult, if not impossible, to find any situation, condition, or relationship which does not react to the creative and healing power of love in the mind of man.

It is safe to say that the great intuitions and the great revelations of the ages were correct when they proclaimed that love is the great reality. This we need not accept just because it was said a long time ago. We need but to look at our own lives and experience to verify the fact. And if that is not sufficient, check the psychiatrist or the doctor of psychosomatic medicine. The proofs they can show us of the devastation wrought by the lack of love would make us turn our backs in horror. Although nothing tremendous may have happened to us as the result of our lack of love for all things, our little dislikes and hates are in some way slowly but surely depriving us of the good we may now have, and at the same time are barring us from having more good become a part of our experience.

The Lodestone of Life

It would be unwise to ignore or in any way seek to avoid the greatest of all truths. Love is the lodestone of life and is a feeling that must permeate everything we do and are. It must flow out from us to everyone we contact. And if we are to accept in any degree the evidence of modern investigation we may definitely state that without love there is no living worthwhile, and that even a much larger percentage of physical troubles than we may yet realize is based on the lack of happiness, appreciation, and joy. We must sincerely forgive ourselves for all omissions or lack of love in the past, remove them from our minds now, and replace them with some idea of love that we must discover relative to the previous situation.

Love plays an important part in the life we want to live. It is an essential ingredient. In fact it is a fundamental on which all else is based. Otherwise we would be destroying what we desire faster than we could create it. Love heals, brings peace, and maintains harmony on all levels. Love is the expression of infinite Mind as creation. As we accept this expression in us, as we express love for God, as we let love flow from us into the world about us and let it return to us, as it must, we discover that all else has been included. There is nothing of good that is not encompassed by love. It's the greatest power there is. If we avail ourselves of it, it will serve us well.

In and through all that we do and all that we think, there needs to be a deep feeling of love, an awareness of the interdependence of all things, for this is what makes life what it is.

We are dependent upon God for our existence, and God is dependent upon us for an expression of Himself.

In love alone rests harmonious, constructive action.

16 THE HUMAN EQUATION

There is a destiny which makes us brothers;
None goes his way alone:
All that we send into the lives of others
Comes back into our own.

—EDWIN MARKHAM

Successful living can only occur when we are able to establish harmonious relations with all whom we encounter, whether it be in the home, the office, or on the street corner. We have to have harmonious relationships with all people or we limit our harmonious relationship with any one person. If we limit our abundance in one respect we seem to limit it in all other respects.

The nature of our relationships with others rests upon what we think ourselves to be and what we think the other person is—not superficially, but what we *really* are. Just who do we think we are? Are we responsible for the life that is within us? Are we masterminding this body of ours? Or is there something within and behind what we appear to be that is greater than we are? Of necessity there must be and there is. It is what we are and what the other person is. Each is an individualized expression of the One Mind—God. Regardless of what our outward appearance may be, there is in each of us a spark of the same Divinity.

If once we let ourselves get past the outward appearance of the individual, we come to understand that Life at the center of his being is the same as at the center of our being—Life which is never in conflict with Itself, never in a state of disharmony. We need never view human personality as something unreal or unworthy, but rather as an individualization of the Divine. It is the universal Spirit that is incarnated in each one in a unique way, and that gives warmth, color, and variation to that which otherwise would be an eternal monotony.

Every man should study to be himself, to be his real self, not some fictitious creation of his imagination with which he seeks to clothe himself. He should so live in and from this real self, from the Divine nature within him, that in his relationships with others each shall give and take, and find joy in the giving and taking.

Your Personality

We should have no desire to win friends and influence people or to put on an attractive personality. There is basically nothing we can do to win friends or influence people, nor does the attractive personality come in a package at the corner store. A person who persistently maintains an attitude of love and good-fellowship, having freed himself from undue self-criticism and harshness, will find himself surrounded by friendship, appreciation, and loyalty. And all this is in accord with immutable law. To have friends we first must be a friend. We do not influence people, we cooperate with them. The only personality we can display to the world is our interpretation of the nature of our Divine individuality.

Friendship and all harmonious relationships with others can only be established through love, affection, and kindness. Not the superficial kind, but the real and sincere. It has been demonstrated time and time again that the love of mother for child, brother for brother, man for woman, and person for person, is basic to a normal healthy condition of mind, emotion, and body. Is it not also true that a sense of love, appreciation, and consideration is just as essential in the contacts of our everyday living? It would definitely appear so. To the extent that we know that love and harmony are the nature of God, and permit them to flow through us, to that extent will our relations with others be harmonious.

Eliminate Conflicts

We need to know what we are and then just be ourselves without arrogance, without fear, without timidity; be ourselves in quietness, in confidence, and in peace; and know that we are one with all people. Then we will be fulfilling the law that makes for unity among all people, that establishes love, companionship, and human relations that are productive of joy and fulfillment of mutual endeavor.

This does not mean that we will ever have to settle for anything less than harmony. It does not mean that we believe wrong is right, or that we must come to endure unpleasant situations. It does mean that we are establishing harmony and right relations out of what might appear to be chaos and confusion.

It means that the greater will always supersede the lesser. That love, which is the nature of the Infinite, will always supersede and transcend that which is unlike it. That where enmity may now exist, a love embodied and expressed will replace it. That a life immersed in loneliness can soon be surrounded by friends. That conflict in the home, the office, or at the conference table can be resolved only by that which is greater than conflict—love and harmony which flow from the Divine center of our being, embodied and expressed in our environment.

Sound relations with others do not permit of any selfishness. What good we may desire for ourselves we must also desire for them. Jealousy of others can have no place in our thinking; what we would deprive them of we would be depriving ourselves of. Competition with others is futile, for it implies that there is not enough to go around and we want more than they are getting, therefore we limit what we ourselves may be able to get. The Universe is abundant; we do not need to fight for things in the fear that there is not enough to go around or that we must defeat our neighbor or fellow man in securing our share. Rather, through mutual endeavor a greater joy and fulfillment may be achieved than when each walked alone. Life is one enormous cooperative interrelated creation. As we come to learn to cooperate with Life and our fellow man we are more nearly expressing the order and harmony that reside in the Mind of God.

Cooperation

And where does all of this start? In us. Today. Each is a center of Divine Love. Where do we first learn to express this? In our home. We express love, cooperation, and fellowship, and know and feel the interdependence of every member of our home. Everyone in our home is a Divine being, cooperating with those about him in love, in trust, and in joy. The father and mother stand for the guiding principle, for affection and protection, for care and thoughtfulness—in no arrogant sense whatsoever, but always with a spirit of cooperation. The children, too, are part of the Divine family and each must be considered in the light of his own individuality and all join together for the purpose of experiencing the kingdom of heaven here and now.

The same idea is extended to the community, to the nation, and to the world, until we finally learn to feel that we are a part of Life, that we belong to the world in which we live, and the Universe of which it is a part. Everyone longs for the companionship of those who understand, who in a certain sense melt into his being, while he melts into theirs in common accord and agreement. Love and affection are the greatest things on earth and through their recognition and appreciation they can become the greatest power in any man's life.

Let us not be timid in using the action of love as law. Let us get rid of our hates, past and present. Let us get over our dislikes of others and our pet peeves about our associates. Stop resenting the attitudes of the clients we call on. Eliminate all sense of animosity toward others around the conference table. Stop having petty hurt feelings in the home. Why must we do this? Why must we have peace and harmony in our thinking? Because others can only be to us what we think they will be to us. Because according to the Law of Mind in Action our relationships with others are established by what we think about others. Others can only act toward us the way we would have them act.

Harmonious Relationships

Without any hesitancy, without any delay, we eliminate from our thought all ideas of undesirable relations, past or present. We know that we are an expression of God who knows only love, harmony, and cooperation, and that everyone we encounter is also an expression of God. As we recognize, accept, and permit this creative action of God to flow in and through us, it automatically draws to us the corresponding Divine nature in others, regardless of how much it may appear to be buried or covered up at the moment. The reaction from the other will come—it has to come. We have established a cause; there has to be an effect that will be a reflection of this cause.

The incorporating of a love of others in our life is amazing in the immediate results forthcoming. Even the most cynical will appreciate what will happen. Simplicity, sincerity, and love can break down antagonistic barriers, finally conquer indifference, eliminate coldness and isolation. Our lives depend on the love of God for us, and God depends on us for expression in us, as us, and through us. We in turn are interdependent with all of those about us for the love and harmony that exist between us, for a fuller enjoyment of life and living. This interdependence is one of the most important things that we need to include in every aspect of our lives. It is fundamental and basic.

Think Highly of Yourself

And there is one person that we must learn to get along with above all others. That person is ourself. We must never belittle ourself. Never dislike ourself. Never resent what we are or the way we feel; and stop feeling guilty in any way. God created us, we are His expression. If we have done many things wrong up to this time, if perhaps we have not been all all things we could have been—well, that is the way things are. But the larger possibility is always ahead of us. We can start becoming more of it right now; start moving out of what we are into what we can be. Where we may not previously have recognized the Divinity within us and may have impeded Its expression through us, we now know better. The moment we start to get on good terms with ourself all else will, to fall into place, for then we will be in harmony with God, and God includes us and everything and everyone else.

We learn how to live with others in complete harmony and joy when we come to know that at the center of his being, each is an individualized expression of God.

Each needs to express the Life within him in his own way, but never at the expense of another.

All difficulties and conflicts in our experience may be resolved by love. The greater always supersedes the lesser.

Most of all we need to come into a greater awareness of our own importance to the Mind that created us.

17 HEALTH IS NORMAL

Prayer acts not only on our affective states but also on the physiological processes. Sometimes it cures organic disease in a few instants or a few days.
—ALEXIS CARREL, M.D.

CERTAINLY, in the successful experience of living, health is a prime factor. And in all probability nothing is of more importance, nothing of more immediate concern, than the present state of one's health. Is it good or bad? Is it getting better or worse? "Look at what happened to Joe, could that happen to me?" We wonder, "What new thing will the doctors think up for me to have?" when actually the doctors are in a state of constant amazement as to what patients think up to have happen to themselves!

From a historical viewpoint the idea of a connection between the state of mind and the state of health of the body is anything but new. In *Emotions and Bodily Changes*, a medical book on psychosomatic relationships by Flanders Dunbar, M.D., the following appears at the start of the volume:

> Nearly half a millennium B.C. Socrates came back from army service to report to his Greek countrymen that in one respect the barbarian Thracians were in advance of Greek civilization: They knew that the body could not be cured without the mind.

"This," he continued, "is the reason why the cure of many diseases is unknown to the physicians of Hellas, because they are ignorant of the whole." It was Hippocrates, the Father of Medicine, who said: "In order to cure the human body it is necessary to have a knowledge of whole things." And Paracelsus wrote: "True medicine only arises from the creative knowledge of the last and deepest powers of the whole universe; only he who grasps the innermost nature of man, can cure him in earnest."

Our Amazing Body

That the body is a wonderful mechanism there is no doubt, but how many of us have realized just how amazing it is? One of its most unique features is the fact that it is made up of dynamic material. Why do we say it is dynamic? Powerful muscles that are relaxed may be called into violent action by a minute amount of energy coursing along nerve pathways. Whether the temperature outside the body is 120° above zero or 30° below zero the body readily adapts itself, maintaining a normal temperature of not more than 98.6°. The eye responds and adapts to a very small amount of light. A foreign particle enters the skin and immediately there is rushed to the area internal materials needed to isolate it, fight infection, and heal the break in the skin. Whether the air is dry or moist the body adjusts itself so that bodily fluids are maintained at a normal level. The heat developed within the body by muscular effort would be damaging beyond repair if a built-in cooling system did not start to function. The body needs oxygen, but whether a person be at sea level or in the oxygen-shy air at a mountaintop, adjustments are made for the body to rightly function.

Not only is adaptability evidenced in relationship to the outer world but in the internal structure and functioning of the body itself. The adaptability that the body appears to have rests entirely on the fact that it is composed of material that is dynamic, material that is readily adapted to a terrific range of conditions and situations.

The Stability Factors

The question then arises: What is it that establishes what might be termed the norm? What maintains the dynamic material of the body in a state of stability? What determines the equilibrium that is evidenced? It would appear that it is not necessarily contained within the material of the body itself, for as we have seen, this is far from stable, is always ready to conform and adapt itself to new stimuli and conditions, and is always ready to start to function in a different manner. Perhaps we need to go back to an idea we encountered earlier. We found that everything in the physical world, animate and inanimate, was the result of some organizing factor, a purposeful activity, a formative element that indicated there was intelligence involved that functioned in accord with law. This is what we encounter in the body. The body, in structure and function, is a mass of dynamic material held together by an intelligent organizing factor, which operates in accord with law.

It has been said that there possibly is not an atom in the body that is over a year old. The body is constantly renewing itself—taking in new material and discarding old. Rebuilding, replacing, repairing. And it is all done in accord with a plan, with a pattern that can only be, as we have seen, an idea, a concept of thought—thought at the spiritual level of creativity, thought in the Mind of Spirit, God.

This ability of the body to maintain its dynamic material at a level of equilibrium was described by famed physiologist Walter B. Cannon as *homeostasis,* which he termed the essential functioning of the autonomic nervous system maintaining a balance of activity in the body. There is that *something* which does seek to regulate and control the body's dynamic material at a normal level in the face of an almost infinite variety of conditions surrounding it and within it. The beauty and wonder of physiological studies is in this action.

Another factor that has always been most impressive to biologists and men of medicine is the ability of the body to cure itself of disease, in order to maintain a stable and constant condition. This natural curative force has long been recognized and was advanced by Hippocrates and termed *vis medicatrix naturae*. When at any time the normal state of the body is upset, there is called forth an activity that attempts to correct the condition. This self-regulatory power of the body was described by a nineteenth-century physiologist in this way: "The cause of every need of a living being is also the cause of the satisfaction of the need."

The Curative Power

It is only through the existence of the factors of equilibrium, *homeostasis,* and *vis medicatrix naturae* that the men of medicine can help to correct an undesirable bodily condition. Doctors can assist, supply aids, remove obstacles, and perform many other corrective measures, but after they have done all they can do they must wait. They wait for the body to re-establish itself in equilibrium. They wait for the normal natural curative forces of the body to take over and assert themselves. The physician cannot make a cut heal, cannot make new skin, cannot make a new organ. He can only pave the way for corrective action on the part of the body. This action by the body is accomplished through the manifestation of the invisible pattern or organizing factor in and through the dynamic material of which the body is composed. And this intelligent force would have to be consistent or life could never have maintained itself.

Your Thinking and Health

To what degree are we, as thinking entities, capable of creative thought, able in any way to disrupt the flow of the organizing factor in and through us? The answer would appear to be much more than we realize—different authorities vary. Some say fifty percent of our ailments are self-induced by the way we think, others say seventy-five percent, still others say ninety percent. Almost every type and condition of illness has been in some way or other related to our pattern of thinking, a pattern of thinking that apparently is contradictory to the spiritual pattern of a perfect and healthy body.

This is so often evidenced by our doctor's admonitions to relax, don't worry, don't be fearful. What is he trying to tell us? He knows that a disturbed mind causes havoc in the body, a havoc he can see and measure. But is there not a larger implication in his words, one that perhaps he is not always fully aware of? He knows the obvious results of the disturbed mind, but what about the extent and degree of our negative thought patterns that block the expression in us of that perfect spiritual pattern which created us to begin with and which seeks to maintain and sustain us?

Cancer, tuberculosis, kidney and liver diseases, arthritis, heart conditions—name it and some medical investigator has discovered a relationship between the ailment and a pattern of thought. But what about those infectious diseases that enter the body from the outside? The answer is that there has been an overwhelming exposure or that the body has been mentally preconditioned so that it was receptive to infection, becoming a fertile breeding ground for it.

Pills and Prayers

Without realizing it far too many people are slowly committing suicide through the way they think, through establishing within themselves patterns of thought that inhibit or prevent the flow of Life in and through them. With every pill we have prescribed for us we should also be given a suggested creative prayer, a suggested way to correct our destructive patterns of thought. The truth of this statement has been discovered in the fact that a medicine that theoretically always should work, may not. Not through any fault of the medicine but because the patient does not think it will work, or he unconsciously does not want it to work. Similarly, sugar pills, placebos, often have as great a curative effect as actual medicine when the patient is not aware of the fact that he is taking sugar pills. He just knows that the pills he is taking are going to make him better, and better he gets. The degree of faith and conviction he has in the pills he should also have in his own mental concept of a cure effected, of health regained.

We must get ourselves and our limited human thinking out of the way so that the Divine pattern of perfection can fully express itself in us. For who can make his own heart beat? What doctor can cause the blood to circulate? All we seem to be able to do through our own efforts is to confuse and confound the operation of Life in us in Its normal natural expression of health and wholeness.

Be Kind to Yourself

We must stop beating ourselves up physically by damaging thoughts, destructive emotions, and unwise physical activity. We must turn from all our worries, anxieties, and fears about our body and know that there is a normal pattern of health, an organizing factor that knows what to do and how to do it— that perfect idea which does exist and which will express and manifest in us as us when we recognize it and accept it as doing so. The doctor can assist the body mechanically through surgery and medication; we can assist through how we think and act. We may need to do a little mental surgery on ourselves to remove old patterns of negative thinking which have gotten us into the situation in which we now find ourselves. Then will we be able to have new ideas grow and mature into sound healthy concepts, which will not refuse but which will let us accept without reservation the infinite Wisdom within the body which ever seeks fuller and more complete expression.

The Source of Health

The foundation for any idea that health is a normal state for the body—this is a fact or else the body would never make any attempt to cure itself—rests in the concept that we are living in a perfect Universe, regardless of any appearances to the contrary. Logic and reason, as well as revelation and inspiration, lead us to believe that God is still in His heaven and all would be right with us if we came into harmony with spiritual Reality. This is the teaching of all the great and wise. It is the conclusion and the teaching of those upon whom the hope of the world makes its greatest claim, and we would be wise to follow the pattern of their thought. Whether we fully understand it or not, the *reality* of ourselves is one with God, and anything and everything that appears to be attached to this reality that contradicts the Divine nature, even though we must admit that it is an experience, cannot be the final truth of our being.

In psychological fields it is being said that there must always be an attempt to separate the neurosis from the neurotic. In other words, all the effects of a neurosis, with its morbid fears, its doubts and uncertainties, are merely something which is attached to the real person. If we carry this a little further we can arrive at the conclusion that everything that is wrong with the body is merely a shadow cast across the face of a greater reality—physical health. Apropos of this viewpoint is the statement made by one doctor to the effect that in some cases the personality of the patient is of more importance than the disease process itself. And another was led to say that the speed of a patient's recovery is closely related to the intention, conscious or unconscious, of the patient to recover. All too often it is found that physical invalidism in a person first started as a psychological invalidism, or should we say spiritual infantilism?

Availing oneself of medical knowledge and wisdom, or the

use of creative thought in the form of prayer for the attainment of health, are but different approaches to the same goal—health, which must exist as a spiritual reality. Both are often needed. The medical profession more and more recognizes the value and importance of prayer in the recovery of a patient.

Food for Thought

An interesting sidelight is to be found in an authoritative and widely recognized medical book on psychosomatic medicine. For a long time most people, as well as doctors, have known that warts are often removed through a process of thought—we would say through faith and prayer. In this book we find one medic suggesting that warts be removed in the following manner: "The physician has to take his time, has to be in the proper state of mind, has to concentrate, and has to be convinced of what he is doing." And in another medical handbook we find it mentioned that "psychotherapeutic suggestion" might be of value in the removal of warts.

From one point of view is there any difference between a wart and a cancer of the skin? True, they are different in nature and structure, but are they not the same in that they both are unnatural conditions of the skin? Perhaps the day will come when cancer will be included as well as warts to be treated with prayer and faith. An instance was related in an English medical journal about a doctor who consistently removed warts from children in this manner. A colleague tried it and the result was that the wart on the child's hand did not go away but the doctor got one of his own! Perhaps he thought so much about the wart being there, rather than not being there, that all he did was to create one for himself!

In all processes of spiritual treatment, creative prayer, or affirmative thinking, there must always be a turning away in thought from the appearance, from the evidence of disease. The condition is not ignored, but recognized as something that needs to be changed. There is not a dwelling of thought on the appearance, but instead on the idea of perfection that can and will manifest itself as health. There is nothing that can oppose this expression of health in us unless we permit it to do so. This is comparable to a medical dictum that all thought, conscious or unconscious ideation—psychic energy—seeks adequate bodily expression.

A great many people are concerned about their weight. One person can eat everything in sight and not gain an ounce. Another person only needs to take a good look at a menu and he seems to gain pounds. Wherein is the cause? Is it possible that often a person's body is so conditioned in its functioning by thought patterns that it either will or will not take on weight regardless of the amount or type of food eaten?

Your Main Endeavor

We come to realize that health is our natural, normal state. It is unnecessary to argue with others about this. But to those of us who are desirous of establishing a new way of thinking that will enable us to wholly accept the perfection of health that can exist for each one of us, it is always wise to keep our thought simple and direct. And it will make no difference whether one, a thousand, or ten thousand people argue against our conclusion. Each in simple faith and trust can, if he will, learn to live directly from the inspiration of the moment and by gradually detaching his thought of himself from everything that is negative, prove to himself the correctness of his position through a definite betterment in his living.

In prayer we are not concerned with illness, sickness, and disease; but with their opposites, health, wholeness, and perfection. We are not concerned with skepticism, doubt, or agnosticism; but with their opposites, faith, trust, and belief. We seek to turn entirely from all objective appearances and affirm, even in the midst of extreme bodily confusion, the right action of God in and through the body, the manifestation of the perfect pattern of health, the perfect functioning of the organizing factor.

The Start of Good Health

Better health starts with the knowledge, backed by conviction and belief, that there is One Life, that Life is perfect, and that Life is our life right now. In It is the complete and whole pattern of perfection. We accept without reservation that It is the spiritual reality of our being. It is the only source, the only cause of every perfect action and function in our body. It alone heals and makes whole. Regardless of what the condition may be, It knows what to do, how to do it, and when to do it. Life, Spirit, Intelligence is both what our body is and is the directing and controlling factor that maintains its perfect circulation, assimilation, and elimination. We know and are convinced of the truth of all this. We declare and affirm, without a shred of doubt, that regardless of appearances, regardless of what the situation may be, our body is now conforming to its perfect spiritual pattern; all that is wrong is made right, all that needs to be removed is being removed, all that needs to be restored is being restored. Nothing is barred or withheld from the limitless creative action and power which flow from God.

As we turn in thought to infinite Spirit as the source, and the only source, of our lives, and know It is good and perfect and expresses Itself as goodness and perfection in us, we are turning our thought away from whatever appearances may be. As we turn our thought away from the appearances, there is nothing to support or sustain them. As we continuously affirm the positive and good, we are automatically eliminating the negative, the undesirable. There is no necessity of any negative condition existing within our bodies other than the necessity we ourselves insist upon.

Health is normal and natural.

Life and health exist now; the experience and enjoyment of them begin when we accept them.

The gift has been given; it is up to us to accept it.

As we start to accept we will learn how to accept more and more from the infinite Source of health.

18 MENTAL GROWTH

Unless we now can clear away the venerable rubbish of the past and the bigotries of the present that so confuse our thinking, and discover a common foundation of enlightened belief and faith on which all men can build their own philosophies, we are not worthy of the age in which we live.

—EDMUND W. SINNOTT

MAX PLANCK, the famed physicist and Nobel Prize winner, said that science and religion have a common goal: "On to God!" We might add that philosophy should be included. There should always be a seeking out, a continuing endeavor on the part of each individual to discover the meaning of Life and experience It in every aspect of living.

Of these three approaches to what we have called ultimate Reality, probably the most familiar is that of religion, which has been defined as a man's belief in God or gods. And since there are such varied interpretations of basic religious concepts, which fundamentally may be quite similar, naturally there is and always has been a great variance between professed religious beliefs.

Arnold Toynbee, famed historian-philosopher, in a critical analysis of the world's seven great living religions has discerned that if they are shorn of the adornments with which they have clothed themselves during the centuries there are certain fundamentals common to them all. He feels that these basic truths will far outlive any dogmatic consideration of them. Outstanding is the fact that the seven great religions of the world recognize a spiritual Presence in the universe, something that is greater than man, which is spiritual Reality, absolute Reality, and that It is good. These religions also recognize that there is a need within man to become aware of this Reality, to be in touch with It and in harmony with It. It is only in this way that man can feel at home in the world in which he finds himself.

Six of the religions hold that spiritual Reality also has a very personal aspect, personal in the sense that a human self is personal, and that in this manifestation of It human beings have encounters with It. There is also the fact that these great religions recognize that this spiritual Reality has an impersonal aspect, which we have designated as Law.

Religion, for us, should include whatever revelation is valid and whatever the deep spiritual experience of the ages has taught us.

As for philosophy, it may be considered to be anyone's opinion about anything. This is why philosophers have the privilege to disagree with each other. Philosophy, then, unlike science, may or may not be based on verifiable principles. It may or may not be true. It is but an individual's effort, by what he terms the logic of his thought, to explain the nature of things as they are.

On the other hand, science deals with laws or principles, with the way they work, and how to use them. Therefore science is a very impersonal study. It claims no special dispensations of Providence and no Divine revelations of truth other than the revelation of laws.

It is from the combination of these three fields that we gather such knowledge as we have. In our approach to a science of mind, to the creative use of our thought in prayer, we have sought to combine these three methods of thinking. As a result we have discovered that we have two basic principles: a Divine Presence which is God the living Spirit, Mind, Intelligence; and universal Law, action and reaction, upon which rests the dependability of all scientific investigation. We should expect, then, to find, even in what has developed into our own philosophy, the need of combining our deep intuitive feelings with our knowledge of a universe of law and order.

Facts and Faith

Such a philosophy may be designated as modern metaphysics. In considering modern metaphysics Omar John Fareed, M.D., has written: ". . . metaphysical teachings present a tolerant, dynamic religious faith. I believe in faith. If we eliminate doubt, we get a greater impact from that which is our true self. In other words, this true self is a part of the Whole and has access to the creative power of the Whole . . ."

Physics and metaphysics do not contradict each other. Fact and faith need never collide. When they appear to, either the faith is misplaced or the fact misinterpreted.

Scientists know they are using a law correctly when they are able to secure repetitive results; and in the same way they verify the action of the law they assume must exist. To ascertain and verify the more subtle laws of nature is not always an easy thing. Einstein, during much of his later life, was endeavoring to finish the formulation of his unified field theory. He did not achieve the final result he desired, the complete explanation by one formula of nature's three basic fields of energy—gravitation, magnetism, and electricity. However, more recently Werner Heisenberg, German physicist and Nobel Prize winner, feels that he has been able to develop such a theory that is workable and possesses basic simplicity and mathematical beauty. To a question properly put to nature there is always a simple and direct answer.

We have to verify for ourselves the Law of Mind. If we say

a law works in a certain way and we use it accordingly and it produces a desired result, can we do other than assume that such a law does exist? However, in the use of creative prayer, just as in any scientific laboratory experiment, does not a great responsibility rest upon the shoulders of the individual to carefully and properly perform the undertaking?

Think Carefully

In science and metaphysics we are dealing with intangibles, and the laws of both are but concepts and will forever remain such, being our interpretation of an aspect of the nature of Reality. At the present time we may feel that in our use of the Law of Mind we are dealing with something that is a little more subtle than the physical laws of science. This could only be because of our unfamiliarity with it. All laws are of the same intangible nature but just as definite and positive. In creative prayer there is no reason why we should not be just as careful and meticulous of the process that goes on in our minds as the physicist who checks and rechecks his laboratory procedures and eliminates all external and extraneous factors which would prevent the success of that which he is undertaking.

The Law of Mind works for all people all the time and many specifically direct this action. More and more people are coming to realize Its nature and practical application in everyday living. The fact that Its positive application is valid in a great many lives gives evidence that It must of necessity have to work that way in the life of everyone who so applies It.

Regardless of what is discovered as fundamental to science or intuitively ascertained as basic to religion, both pertain to the same Reality, the nature of things as they are. There must always be a continuing discovery of more of the nature of God. So we find ourselves individually in the position of ascertaining through inspiration, feeling, and knowledge that thought is the creative factor in our lives. That our word is acted upon by a Power that is greater than we are. We have every right to believe in the immutable action of Law. And all sense of holding thoughts or of mental concentration must be supplanted with the idea of loosing thought into the action of Law. All sense of compulsion is withdrawn and supplanted with a sense of cooperation. All sense of coercion or personal will power is withdrawn and supplanted with the idea of willingness, of letting, of permitting.

When one is able to achieve and maintain this attitude he finds that he has the same attitude that is behind any scientific investigation. His own personal choice ceases with his conviction in an idea; then the Law takes over. But he may always use his personal choice to establish a new conviction resulting in a new reaction in the Law. Therefore there is a sense of relaxation, a sense of letting go, a sense of freedom.

To a great degree the larger potential for us rests in our being able to do just this. We make it possible by providing the channel for its expression as we recognize it, accept it, and use it. Our new design for living comes to pass as an automatic reaction. Ours is the thinking, the knowing, the accepting. The creation of it is the normal natural activity of Law in God's universe of order and harmony.

The Endless Search

Just as there has been a continual growth of knowledge and wisdom on the part of the human race there is inherent within each individual the possibility of progression. And it would appear that regardless of what or how much we may be able to learn about the nature of our own mind and consciousness and the laws relative to their action, there will always be more to be known. The more we seem to know only reveals the more that is to be known. Our spiritual growth would appear to be something without end, an ever greater expression of what we already are.

In reference to the idea that man must continually progress philosopher Ralph Tyler Flewelling has written: "More profound still is the insight that every flash of genius, every stirring of understanding, every expression of love and sacrifice is due to the inspiration and [incarnation] of the Creative Spirit, on which the whole cosmos depends."

In the pursuit of science, as well as in any pursuit which reveals more of the laws of nature, we should expect a continual growth. Everything is not yet known about electrical energy, and the knowledge still to be gained far surpasses that already known. So in our use of the science of mind we must never feel that the last word has been spoken. No final word ever will be spoken.

One of the most terrible things to contemplate would be to consider ourselves as eternal beings without at the same time thinking of such eternality as being an everlasting unfoldment. The universe is not a static thing forever reproducing itself in exactly the same way. Neither is it something that was wound up, left to its own devices, and is now running down. It is, rather, a vast and infinite potential which, while it must ever remain true to the laws of its nature, will always be manifesting itself in infinite variations.

Regardless of how much or how little we may know today, what we do now know is but a steppingstone to a greater knowledge. There is always the more yet to be. We should have an enthusiastic spirit of adventure toward the endless discovery of what we are. There would be no fun in life unless this were true, no joy in living and no incentive in accomplishment unless there were a possibility of growth.

Make All Things New

In actual practical experience this can mean the creation of a new experience in living. In every creative prayer we make we should expect to transcend any previous moment of creative thought we have ever had. This increased spiritual endeavor should be a part of our whole mental and emotional setup and background. It will lend the zest of adventure, the incentive of accomplishment, and the enthusiasm of expectation. And this will always be based on the calm, dispassionate concept that there are two fundamental aspects of Reality which neither science, philosophy, nor religion can change: first, the concept of a Divine Presence overshadowing and indwelling everything; and second, the realization of Law as the way It creates and governs. Upon these two premises everything that we have accomplished or can accomplish is based. These two fundamental propositions will never change but within the realm of their possibility there will forever be ceaseless change, ceaseless differentiation, and every moment will see a new birth from the unborn into the born.

So in our own growth, spiritually, and in the fuller experiencing of Life Itself, we are in a certain sense like an artist setting up our canvas to paint a new scene. The basic colors and pigments, the canvas and the easel and the brushes will be the ones we used yesterday. But who knows what new picture will be precipitated upon the canvas through our creative imagination? Who knows what new inspiration will flow through us to accomplish something new and different? Thus every moment is a fresh starting point, unconditioned by anything that has ever existed, something being born here and now.

The continuing challenge is to increase our knowledge of the infinite potential which lies ahead of us, and every increase but reveals the more that is to be known.

To realize that an infinite Artist, the Divine Creator, the Cosmic Reality is back of and in and through all of our acts is to realize the truth which enables us to enter with joy and enthusiasm into the day in which we live.

Each day is a new creation, a new moment for a fuller awareness of spiritual Reality, and a time for designing the new life we want to live.

19 THE LARGER LIFE

> *We know the truth when we see it, let skeptic and scoffer say what they choose. . . . Our faith comes in moments . . . yet is there a depth in those brief moments which constrains us to ascribe more reality to them than to all other experiences.*
>
> —EMERSON

IT MAY SEEM SHOCKING to say that the only God we can ever know will be discovered within ourselves. Our first reaction to such a concept might cause us to feel that it is blasphemous, that we are causing the individual life to usurp the throne of the Almighty and the prerogatives of the Infinite. But such is not the case. Any drop of water in the ocean is still the ocean as that drop, but the drop of water is not all the ocean. So any individual life is God manifesting in, as, and through that individual at the level of that individual's awareness of God.

In spite of the fact that all of the great mystics have said in effect, "The Father and I are one," why do we find this idea so difficult to comprehend? They have all said that we are one with all life, one with all that God is, yet for the most part organized religion has taught that there is man *and* God, as though man were something separate and apart from Reality. Regardless of what we may have read or may have been taught, we can never meet a bigger or a greater God than the one we can conceive of in our own thought. All too often we have a God created in man's image rather than man created in God's image, hence we wind up with a very limited idea of God and we ourselves become an image of our own limited thinking about God. We have created a picture, stepped into it, and been entrapped by it.

When we say that the only God we will ever know we will discover within ourselves, we do not mean that such a God is a figment and creation of our own imagination. But rather that there is an indwelling God manifest through our own personal and individual relationship to the Infinite. In no way does this minimize God, rather it magnifies Him. For how can a person know anything outside himself any more than he can jump away from his own shadow? The indwelling God is the greatest single factor in our whole lives. It means that there is nothing between us and God, there is no intermediary, there is no place to go to find God. God already exists in the midst of us and if we would try to seek Him elsewhere it would be like God trying to hunt for Himself. God is not lost, and neither are we lost or separated from God. The more completely we are able to see God in everything, the more completely will the One God in all things respond to us.

Psychologist Gordon Allport has said, "A man's religion is the audacious bid he makes to bind himself to creation and to the Creator. It is his ultimate attempt to enlarge and to complete his own personality by finding the supreme context in which he rightly belongs." We do not create the God who responds to us, but rather we are so extending and deepening our own vision that we are beginning to understand that the response to us is by correspondence to our mental attitudes. In this way God does not increase, but we do.

Accept Life

For these reasons we have said that effective prayer, creative thought, should be a matter of declaration and acceptance, not a petition, a supplication, a begging. If we petition or beg what are we doing but attempting to make God prove that He is God! We would appear to be questioning God, expressing doubt as to His nature and reality. There would appear to be a complete lack of faith on our part.

We have to grow up and mature in this matter of faith. We need not so much to have faith *in* God as we need to have the faith *of* God. But when we petition God in a prayer we are expressing a hope that there will be a response, we are not expressing the faith of God. On the other hand, when our prayers take the form of declaration and acceptance we then have the faith of God, the faith God has in His own word and in His own creation.

As we are able to grow in this respect we will discover that we are growing in what has been the secret of spiritual power through the ages, and this will be the secret of the power of our word, prayer, or treatment. For God is in everything. One Essence is diffused through all things. One Presence incarnated in everyone, seeking expression through him. Philosopher William Ernest Hocking has said that every word we speak is a new incarnation of God.

All of this may contradict popular theories, the materialistic philosophies, and the theologies that are based on the disunion of man and God, but it will never contradict the greatest revelations of the ages, the highest intuitions of man, the current trends of modern science, or the basic fact that there is but one final Power in the universe, present everywhere, which when recognized may be consciously directed in our experience.

The Urge Within

The person who has the deepest concept and awareness of God, of the Spirit dwelling within him, will be the one who will be able to do the most with the creative power of his thought. In this respect we will always be maturing and growing up, always becoming more God-like in our natures and actions. Just as life is made to live, and there is no song until someone sings it, so God remains unreal to us until we have made Him real. There is always the Divine urge within us, that presses against us from within seeking our recognition of Itself. God is always declaring Himself as what we are but we need to have the desire to wake up, grow up, recognize and become aware of what we are.

It is today that we must learn to live. And when we do, tomorrow will take care of itself even though it is born out of today. We should be certain that today, well lived, will produce a better tomorrow, *ad infinitum*. Have we grown a little today? Have we created a better design for tomorrow? Have our faith and our understanding deepened? Is our expectation broader? Is our love more inclusive? Have we demonstrated a little more effectively that our thought can be creative of good? If so, the future will take care of itself.

We should not allow ourselves to get confused over abstract ideas to the extent that we lose the possibility of getting the most out of life. With a simple faith and conviction we need to see God more completely in His creation. We must look a little more deeply into our own nature and the nature of others so that God inherent or incarnate in all things becomes more revealed to us. This is our only problem, today or any day, and we should ever endeavor to reduce it to its utmost simplicity rather than try to see how profound or abstract we can make it.

Important Things in Life

There was a time when everyone believed the world was flat. This belief was so universally entertained that everyone's reasoning was based on the conception of a flat world. It was not until someone broke down the old pattern of thought that a new conception could take its place. The new concept did not create a round world but it did hasten the possibility of people's experiencing it. And so it is with everything in life. We should always be breaking down old patterns of thought and creating new ones out of a greater vision.

The question that presents itself, then, is how are we going to know whether or not during this process we are sometimes discarding a truth and accepting a fallacy? This no man can answer with absolute certainty but must depend upon experience, a sort of trial and error method, in which he ascertains the veracity of his new ideas.

But we do have a certain criterion or method of procedure based on a deep inward knowingness that we all possess, a sort of transcendent wisdom we are born with. For instance, we know that Life *is* because we are alive. We know that there must be a creative Reality behind the universe else it would not be here. We know there must be a personalness in the universe else we would not be persons. Consequently, if we think back within our consciousness to that Something greater than our experience, we do actually contact that Something because It exists and is what we are.

Through a silent contemplation, which is always good for anyone, we can come to ascertain the rightness of all the good things in our lives. Take the idea of love. It is always good to dwell on the thought of love and what it means, what must be the great attribute of love in the Universe which endlessly gives of Itself to Its creation. Love implies a givingness, a sharing, a communion of spirit. As one dwells on this idea, he finds that his own consciousness of love, of affection, of compassion, and of well-wishing increases until he finally sees that it is impossible for him to come into the fulfillment of his destiny until he has learned to embrace all life.

It is the same with the idea of peace, beauty, or happiness. To meditate silently and with feeling on these ideas is to enter more completely into a realization of their meaning. Here is where faith plays such an important role, for faith in the Invisible, faith in God, is not some wild and idle dream of an empty-headed idealist. It is the first and most important thing in life. To learn to be at home in the Universe, to not be

afraid of It, to live and think and act as though It were not a
hostile force but a friendly Presence forever embracing us,
is the beginning of right thinking, the beginning of all wisdom,
the starting point of everything that is worthwhile.

You Are Not Alone

Achievement of growth in the right direction is not a solitary
endeavor. The man who tries to live unto himself alone will
soon become very lonely. He will find that he has isolated himself from the greater good he has desired. He will discover that
he has separated himself from the central meaning and action
of life; and when he does this he will find that he has excluded the highest gift of heaven.

What we believe and what we profess to have faith in must
not be a casual thing, to be donned one day a week and for-
gotten the rest of the time. Life is in us all the time; we think
all the time; we are continually creating our tomorrows. So
every day, and every moment of every day, we are expressing in
some way or other our faith, beliefs, and convictions. Be sure
of what they are; that they are clear and concise, that they are
practical in everyday living and are demonstrable and workable.

A man is whole only as he experiences wholeness; and science
is discovering that it is impossible for him to experience wholeness within himself until he contacts that Something greater
than he is. No man is whole in isolation, but in inclusion. If
we find a person who deals only with outward facts, we discover
that he is the one who has cut himself off from the possibility
of inspiration, from silent communion with the Divine Presence, and thus has excluded too much that is worthwihle.

The Task Ahead

We should always recognize the significance of facts. But we
should also know that facts may well be interpreted in a new
light and that the law and order we think of in the physical

world should be extended to include the mental and spiritual. This would mean a larger inclusion and with it a larger synthesis. To the matter-of-fact man who bases everything on objective evidence this might seem unwise and unwarranted. On the other hand, we must also realize that it is to those who have had the deeper experience that we look for guidance. They are the ones who have really written the pages of human history and growth. They are the ones who have entered into a deeper communion with Reality, to whom the Invisible has been more real. Yes, it is to those we are most indebted. We should always seek to align ourselves in thought and act with those who sought behind the fact to the Creator of facts, the Coordinator of all laws, and the Presence that is diffused in everything.

Your greater potential? Godward!

What does it hold? The greatest good you can conceive that harms no one.

How do you come to possess it? Thought by thought.

Why is it possible for us to create a new life for ourselves? Because we are part of Life, not separate from It or Its creativity.

20 USING WHAT YOU KNOW

> *Everything in nature happens both mechanically and metaphysically, and the source of the mechanical is in the metaphysical.*
>
> —LEIBNIZ

> *Prayer and propitiation may still influence the course of physical phenomena when directed to these centers.*
>
> —SIR ARTHUR EDDINGTON

WHAT IS IT that we may now feel we know, and how may we use in a practical way with a definiteness and a surety?

For us to use advantageously any knowledge we may have we must have a conviction that it is true. It must be sound and logical. In our minds there must be no maybes, no perhapses, no doubts. Intellectually and emotionally it must be accepted as right and correct. We must have a firm foundation on which to start our operations, not a shaky one. If sometimes there is a conflict between our new ideas and the old ones we already have, this conflict has to be resolved. Decisions have to be made. Which make the most sense, are the most logical, and appear to be the most workable? For thought to be productive in any respect it has to be clear, well defined, simple and direct. Indecisive, vacillating thinking never accomplished anything.

Three Basic Ideas

In the creation of a new design for living we have found three very simple propositions:

1. We are living in a spiritual universe. The ultimate reality is God, Mind, Intelligence, or Spirit. God is both the Creator of all things and is all things.
2. There is an impersonal Law of Mind. This is the aspect of spiritual Reality through which and by the means of which It goes forth into expression. In the Mind of God there is a thought, the thought becomes manifest or tangible in accord with Law. Law is not a thing separate from God but the way and the means of God expressing.
3. God, spiritual Reality, is Presence and Person to each of us individually. God is in the midst of us, is what we are. Infinite Presence becomes personalized at the center of our being, warm, colorful, loving, and joyous.

These three propositions add up to the inescapable conclusion that God is what we are, we are of like nature to God. God is creative. God's thoughts become things in accord with Law. Our consciousness is part of the One Consciousness. Our thought is creative, being an expression and activity of God within us. Our thought is creative at the level of our expression of Life, constructively creative to the degree we recognize its nature and determine the way to use it.

The way to use thought in a beneficial and creative way has been called many different things: affirmative prayer, treatment, creative thought, positive thinking, meditation, spiritual mind treatment. But regardless of the name there is a principle which may be used irrespective of race, place, creed, or religion. It is a universal principle that is available to each and all alike. It is a principle that will work for us and through us in the way that we *believe* it will work.

Four Steps in Creative Thinking

What are requisites for the constructive use of our thought? Experience has shown that usually an effective prayer or spiritual mind treatment in some way incorporates within it these four elements: Recognition, Identification, Declaration, and Acceptance.

But before we discuss these four steps we need to remember that they are but suggestions. They are not hard-and-fast rules that must be followed. One or all four may be used. There is no formula involved, no ritual to repeat. There is only an easy, consistent flow of thought that is convinced of the truth of the content involved. Famed medical researcher Alexis Carrel, in commenting on prayer, wrote: "Prayer should be understood, not as a mere mechanical recitation of formula, but as a mystical elevation, an absorption of consciousness in the contemplation of a principle both permeating and transcending our world."

The manner in which each will be able to use and direct his thought in constructive and beneficial channels will have to be worked out individually. The results forthcoming will verify the rightness of how each uses the creative power of his thought.

There is no time, no place, no condition or situation that is more appropriate than another for the use of thought as affirmative prayer. Prayer has had immediate manifestation, the answer, in the midst of confusion and disaster. It has also had results that came from moments of peace and quiet. Most people have found it helpful to be alone, to be quiet, to be removed from distracting surroundings, to have the mind free of a sense of pressure, worry, and tension.

Let us now consider the four elements that are usually contained in prayer that works, in thought that is creative.

1. *Recognition.* We know that there is One Life, that Life is God. There is One Creator, one creation. One Law.

One Intelligence. One Ultimate Reality. It is good, whole, perfect, complete, harmonious.

2. *Identification.* We identify ourselves with God. "I am that which Thou art, Thou art that which I am." The Father and I are one. There needs to be a conscious, intelligent sensing and feeling of the Divine Presence within and as what we are. We are a creation of God and we are expressing God. There is no separation between us and God, we are one.

3. *Declaration.* There is a definite and specific action and movement of intelligence through thought, word, or idea for some definite purpose or person. Not supplication, wishing, hoping, or begging, but a concrete declaration of fact, a specializing of universal Good in some way. There is definitely established in thought, the spiritual level of cause and creativity, a complete idea. An idea to which we may mentally point and know its reality as though we were pointing to the sun and saying, "There is the sun." We know that such a declaration of an idea is God speaking His word in us, God being an active agent in His own creation.

4. *Acceptance.* We accept our declaration, the word we have spoken, as being manifest now. No delay is involved between this cause and its appearance as effect. We accept that our word, the declaration we have made, is the supreme Intelligence speaking through us, and that according to the nature of the way It works, through Law, our word automatically manifests in accord with Law. And in our acceptance of the reality of this good as a tangible effect in our experience we give thanks that it is so, that as we now believe it is done unto us.

There is nothing involved or complicated in any of this. But it does require a clear mind and direct thinking. No wandering thoughts. How long can we think consistently about one idea? Five seconds? Ten seconds? The only will power or effort involved should be in keeping our attention focused on what we want it to be focused on. This is largely a matter of practice, of habit, in which we can become progressively more efficient.

For some people there is a feeling that just to say that God is all there is, is a prayer or spiritual treatment. This is really not a creative prayer or treatment, but rather a preliminary to one, a sort of getting one's consciousness focused on God. This is only a first step, a recognition. To say "There is One Life and that Life is God" does not become a treatment until this idea is connected with the person, situation, or condition for which the treatment is given.

It must always be remembered that our word or treatment, the declaration of the spiritual reality of our idea, is acted upon by a Power greater than we are; acted upon by the infinite creative Intelligence at the level of the belief and conviction we have in the words we have spoken. There needs to be in our consciousness, back of the words we speak, a complete conviction that there is One Life flowing through everything, never congested, never caught in any form of negation.

In affirmative prayer or spiritual mind treatment we must realize that there will always be an automatic reaction to the word spoken and declared at the level of the feeling and conviction embodied in it. That the one who prays does not really make anything happen, he merely provides the channel through which things must happen. This is the meaning of the Law and the Word. The Word is spoken spontaneously while the Law reacts mathematically. How could we ever expect anything to come out of a prayer or treatment unless it was already embodied in it, in thought, in meaning, and in clarity of conviction?

The Great Experiment

Let us look at the whole nature of creative thought from another angle. Every treatment one gives is in a certain sense an experiment with a principle which will never fail to operate.

The principle, being always present and always powerful, both omnipresent and omnipotent, will always respond to us at the level of our conviction. And It will also of necessity respond in the manner and the form of the conviction. Therefore an effective prayer, a spiritual mind treatment, is a definite and a specific thing. Consequently every prayer in a certain sense is a process whereby one acquaints his own consciousness with the reality of what he says, of the *word* he speaks, whether it be for himself or someone else, or some situation or condition. Any such prayer or treatment could fulfill its purpose instantly, and the possibility for this forever exists.

The experiment then lies basically in what degree do we recognize and know that this moment is absolute, is the eternal now, the only moment the Infinite ever knows? The Power is ready and willing, Law always functions; the Presence is perfect and is within us, and Life is complete and whole. Any particular treatment is merely a working with these ideas until a proper conclusion or acceptance of them is accomplished. When one understands this he will also see why it is that people who pray with great faith are the ones who receive a definite answer because they have a complete conviction.

Spontaneous Creativity

In our approach to effective prayer or spiritual mind treatment we must not allow ourselves to become too involved with rules, regulations, procedures, and concepts of the way it must be done. There are certain basic attitudes which are essential but beyond this each is on his own. Prayer and treatment should be entered into with a light spirit, a sense of freedom and happiness, just as children enter into play or into a game. There is a lightheartedness, a delight, a sense of fun, sheer exuberance in the joy of living. We need have no feeling of solemnity, no sense of dealing with heavy and ponderous ideas, or of laborious work to be done. But there should be appreciation and thanksgiving for God's gift to us of the ability to think and of the creativity of our thought.

If we pay too much attention to possible rules or regulations we may establish for ourselves, or accept from others, we will have missed the point of the whole way of prayer. Unless we enter into and possess the spirit of the thing we will gain little. The life will be gone from our words. The word we speak, the idea we declare, the thought we desire to become thing, must spring spontaneously from the heart, be vitally known and experienced in every corner of our mind, be vibrantly felt with every part of our being.

There Are Always Results

Creative prayer is intelligent knowing coupled with emotional conviction. Many prayers have been fully and completely answered for people who might be said to be unlettered—who knew nothing about science, philosophy, or dogmatic religion. They just *knew* God is. Just *knew* prayer always had an answer, and *it always did.* But those of us who have started to toy with ideas, who raise questions which we are not always able to answer, we are the ones who have to pull ourselves together, round up the loose ends of our thought, organize what it is we believe and why we believe it, and then proceed to lift ourselves up to a logical, consistent level of belief and conviction. We have to re-educate ourselves, to discover within ourselves the knowledge that this is God's world we are living in, that it is good, that we are a part of it, and that the answer to every prayer is in the prayer itself, that every thought we have is creative in that it is both cause and effect.

What to Do

Wherein do we use what we know in connection with our everyday living? There is no good thing for which we may not

apply the creative power of our thought as prayer. Nothing is
exempt. Nothing is forbidden. It is equally applicable to all
things, situations, conditions, and relationships.

As for our new design for living, this is established in the
third of the four requisites we mentioned as important for the
effectiveness of creative thought as prayer: the declaration.
Whether we desire health, success, happiness, joy, friendship,
or anything else to make our lives fuller and more complete,
we must first establish them as spiritual realities in our thought,
declare them as existing for us right now. We affirm them as
being our experience as the result of the creative action of God
as Law on the word we speak; our word manifesting at the level
of our understanding of God.

We are always affirming something. We affirm we are sick
or well, unhappy or happy, that we lack or have abundance.
We are always affirming, but now we know what it is necessary
to affirm and declare in order to have life be a joy instead of a
burden.

Learn to Be Definite

In this respect a spiritual mind treatment must be definite
and concise. We must think clearly. Clear thinking may mean
a logical and specific development of an idea to a conclusion,
or it could mean any process of thought that is unruffled or
undisturbed by ideas extraneous to it. How clearly do we really
think?

In the process of giving a spiritual mind treatment for Mary
Jones we perhaps may have the following experience: "There
is One Life, that Life is God, that Life is perfect, and that Life
is Mary Jones' life now. Mary certainly needs it . . . She didn't
look so well the other day, especially in that dress she had on
. . . Wonder where she got it . . . One would think her husband would tell her about it . . . but even he doesn't have
such good taste . . . those awful ties he wears . . . Now where
was I? . . . Oh, yes . . . Mary Jones is a perfect idea in the

Mind of God . . ." *ad infinitum.* We all encounter this in our thinking. But what are we declaring? What direction are we giving our words and the action of the Law? It would be most difficult to say except that Mary Jones' husband would probably buy even worse ties than he now buys. How confused can we get?

What Are You Definite About?

On the other hand, how clearly we think when we have an ache or a pain! Often there is nothing else we can think of, no outside idea seems to be able to enter our minds. Our thought is intent only on how miserable we are, how bad the pain is, how sick we feel. Here there is no wavering, no inconsistency in the direction we are giving the Law. We are specific, definite, and concise. These things we know, and know without a shadow of doubt. This same condition of definiteness seems to apply to many other aspects of our living. If we are poor, poverty is the only thing we can think of. If we are a failure, failure is all we know. What dramatic demonstrations of the way the Law works! What accurate responses we get from our declarations! The detail with which our lives conform to the mental designs we have is amazing. The Law works! But all this is in reverse!

We need to teach ourselves to think just as consistently, just as emphatically, about the things we do want. We must declare for ourselves, in no uncertain terms, the good things of life we desire. And in between the times we set aside for this purpose there must be no backsliding, no letting down of the barriers we have raised against negative ideas. A "yes" one moment and a "no" the next will hold us in the very position we want to get out of.

Clear Thinking

To further expand the idea that a spiritual mind treatment involves clear thinking, we start with the basic principle that

God is all there is and is ever present. Because there is only this One Life, God is now in and through the condition we are working for. There is only One Mind acting in and through everything we declare in our prayer or treatment at the level of our conviction. This action we call Law. Its reaction to us is always at the level of our action in It. We must completely accept that there is such a principle of Mind-action and that this is the way It works, if we are to free ourselves from any existing negative circumstance.

It is impossible to say too much about the necessity of the declaration made in a prayer or treatment being a *real conviction* in the consciousness of the one making it, a *complete belief* in the truth of the statements.

Convince Yourself

In the process of spiritual treatment we have no one to convince but ourselves. The treatment takes place entirely in the consciousness of the individual actively engaged in the definite endeavor of seeking a better life for himself.

Therefore, in actual practice, having first learned the basic technique, the possible procedure, and the vital elements, one closes all the books and turns to himself and pours his whole being, all his wisdom and feeling, into the words of his treatment. He himself becomes the teacher of his own consciousness, the stimulator of his own thought, simply because he cannot live outside or away from himself.

Effective spiritual mind treatment demands clear and specific thinking about the nature of God, our identification with this Reality, the declaration of the good we desire, and the unqualified acceptance of it in and as our experience now.

21 FACING FACTS

*. . . it is indispensable that in all existing
things there must be an active cause, and a
passive subject; and that the active cause is
the intellect of the universe. . . .*

—PHILO

WE MUST ALWAYS be honest with ourselves. We must never
deny the testimony of our senses or doubt the veracity of our
thought. The facts of our experience are real enough.

In our approach to and use of spiritual mind treatment we
do not fool ourselves by saying that no one is ill, no condition
is discordant, the bank account is not low, or that nothing
needs any attention. If someone were not sick we would not
try to cure him. If conditions did not need changing we would
not be trying to improve them. If appearances are other than
they should be, we recognize this fact. We start to do something
about them. To pray for things to get better, if we say there is
nothing wrong, is both a foolish gesture and a waste of time.
Prayer works at the level of causation and from it something
new can go forth into creation as effect creating the wrong
situation.

It is also to be remembered that the offices of prayer and
spiritual mind treatment are not used as a method whereby
we may learn to endure negative conditions, as though there
were some power giving us the grace to live in the midst of

unhappy and painful circumstances. Spiritual mind treatment accomplishes nothing, prayer is not effective, unless it changes the undesirable condition to which it is directed. Signs must follow our belief or else we go around and around in a negative circle. Unless the one practicing the use of creative thought as affirmative prayer or spiritual mind treatment can, as a result of what he does inwardly to his own consciousness, see a direct and specific outward result, he is merely voicing empty words.

This does not mean that the result will have to be instantaneous, although it could be. It does mean that there should be from the very start enough of a definite sign or change taking place so that one may know he is on the right track. If one is treating a case of high blood pressure in himself or another and he has affirmed in his work that the blood pressure is perfectly normal and natural, there should be no hesitation in having a physician check it. The proper treatment or prayer has been given or it hasn't. Perhaps there will need to be a cumulative effect, a gradual building up of a greater faith and conviction. But to be reluctant to have the blood pressure checked would be to suppose that the treatment was based on superstition or that there was nothing that needed to be changed!

Things Must Get Better

In the use of spiritual mind treatment for better health there need never be any hesitation in permitting, or even encouraging a physical examination or checkup by a physician. If the spiritual treatment work is rightly done there will be a continual definite change for the better in the diagnosis. This does not mean that the diagnosis was wrong, for the diagnosis deals with effects and the one giving the spiritual treatment is dealing with cause at the spiritual level which can change the effects.

Treatment work properly done, prayer that is effective, must of necessity produce real results or effects. Not imaginary ones, but tangible ones that can be weighed, measured, and experienced. Unless there is some indication or manifestation of the results of treatment, we have not done our work properly. In that event we start again and continue, persistently and consistently, until we do convince ourselves of the truth that Life in all Its perfection is now our life, or that all the good we seek is now our experience.

In all endeavor of this kind we must always learn to keep our minds as free as possible from the fear or the pain or the uncertainty and confusion that exist in the realm of effects. We must learn to avoid this trap. If we do not watch ourselves we become so immersed in the picture we want to change that we are somewhat helpless. In either praying for ourselves or another we must always *know* that there is that Divine center within us which is never disturbed, never confused; and it is from this center that we seek the motivation for our thoughts and feelings so that we may rise above that in which we outwardly seem to be embroiled.

Hidden Facts

Probably the most difficult of all facts to discover and to face are those within ourselves—to recognize within our own thought the way it has been negatively productive. In all probability we are not even aware of what we have been and are now doing to ourselves. We have to have the courage to look in the mirror of our negative experience and discover in our thought what corresponds to it.

The position in which we may find ourselves is much like that of certain kindergarten children. When disciplinary measures such as sitting on a chair or standing in a corner fail, the teacher has a last resort. She has the child stand and then proceeds to draw a circle on the floor about him with a piece of chalk and tells him that he cannot get out of it. For some reason or other he is unable to, try as he might. He will even try erasing the circle with a handkerchief or his shirttail. But step out of it he cannot.

Perhaps we have to discover the circles of limitation we have drawn about ourselves, across which we seem unable to move.

How many have we drawn? What kind of circles are they?
Do they relate to health, abundance, or happiness? This we
have to discover for ourselves. In any event we face the task of
finding in our patterns of thought the negative content and proceed to do something about it. Establish new ideas, new forms
of declarations, new designs for living.

This is always the great experiment, always the continuing
experiment in the use of affirmative prayer, spiritual mind
treatment. To see how we may, through whatever method we
use, more completely convince ourselves that there is a Divine
and perfect pattern at the center of everything, and that the
Law acting on our word will remove every obstruction until
that which was already there is revealed. Our word projects new
conditions through the same power that made the old ones.

How to Help Others

The question is frequently asked: What should we try to
heal? or, What kind of results or demonstrations should we
try to seek through spiritual mind treatment? Spiritual mind
healing will help anyone, no matter what the condition, if it
is rightly used. It will tend to change any situation, no matter
how desperate it may appear, if it is rightly applied. Spiritual
mind treatment is able to do this because it deals with a transcendent Power working through the human mind.

In this respect there is no difference between working for
oneself or another. Distance means nothing. When one thinks,
he is thinking with the mind within him which is an expression
and individualization of the One Mind. The One Mind is
everywhere present. What you may know and declare in your
mind as the truth about Mary Jones is also known in Mind as
the truth about her. It makes no difference whether Mary Jones
knows that anyone is praying for her or not. But she experiences
the result—she is now better than she was before. Life is more
fully expressing in and through her. Where there was depression of thought there is now a joyousness; where things may
have appeared hopeless there is now a bright future.

The position of one working for another is not a position

of personal responsibility as though he himself were trying to make something happen. But it is a personal responsibility in that he has agreed to try to help someone. There is a vast difference. If we were asked to plow up a corn field and plant wheat in its place we would have taken on a personal obligation to do a certain specific bit of work. But we could not become responsible for the wheat growing. Our agreement and obligation was in dealing with the laws of nature in such a way that they would produce wheat instead of corn.

It is always God, the Power greater than we are that gives the increase. This is just as true in any of the physical sciences as it is in the science of mind, for the science of mind does not exist outside, but within the laws of nature; it is part of them.

Now, we are not asked to plow up a field of corn and plant a field of wheat. We are asked to uproot thoughts and beliefs and ideas and to supplant them with new ones. That this may not seem quite so simple is because we have not fully realized how identical the process is. For too long we have been separating what we call the spiritual or mental from what we call the physical or material. As we have seen, there is no separation. And this is where we so often make our big mistake. We forget that they are all parts of one great Reality.

Uprooting the Undesirable

In the plowing-up process, in our use of the science of mind, we may use several methods to uproot the old. We may make a flat denial of the necessity of the condition or appearance and an equally flat affirmation of the opposite; or we may possibly just use what is called a process of realization. The method used is of no importance whatsoever, provided it produces the desired change.

Basically, whether it be a matter of treating ourselves or another for better health, better conditions, or greater abundance, the process is the same. The mind of the person doing the treating is cleared, uprooted of all ideas contrary to the ones he desires to plant. The new planting that is done, the new declarations that are made, may be for the benefit of his own back yard or that of another. But it all happens in his own mind, his own consciousness.

The way of the plowing up and the planting, the elimination of negative ideas and the implanting of a more desirable ones, each individual must work out for himself. But in the method used there must always be a conformity with the way the Law works; no procedure of any kind can be effective unless it complies with the laws governing it. In other words, we do not arrive by contradicting or opposing the laws of nature, but by agreeing with them.

The only means by which we help ourselves or another is through our mind and its process of thought as part of the One Mind; the only medium through which our thought is creative is that of Law. Mind and Its action as Law is universal; each person is immersed in It, and a thought, prayer, or declaration made in our mind, part of the One Mind, for another at a place removed from us in space, is just as effective, just as creative as though it were for ourselves. In Mind there is no time, no space, no place; there is only wholeness, oneness, and eternity.

Of one thing we must be most certain: that our experience and the world about us are real; we need not disillusion ourselves about this in any way.

We must always be honest with ourselves about our prayers. If we have prayed aright there are specific and tangible results which can and should be verified.

Appearances are effects subject to change, a change in accord with a new cause—a new pattern of thought in the spiritual realm which is in no way limited.

We may help another because of the fact that when we think we are thinking with the One Mind in which everyone is united; that the good we know for another is known in Mind for that person and becomes his experience.

22 DESIGNING A NEW LIFE

Man will hereafter be called to account for depriving himself of the good things which the world lawfully allows.

—ABBA ARIKA

THAT THERE IS a science of right thinking there is no doubt. We have encountered much evidence for the basis of it and the way it works. The reason that we term the use of creative thought a science is the fact that it can be taught, it can be learned, it can be consciously applied with a certainty of definite and repeatable results. This is what we mean when we say there is a "science of mind."

From our point of view no one has any more ability in this respect than another. No one has any more power to use his thought in a creative way than another. We always need to guard against superstition, for it is so easy for the little truth we know to be clothed by so much superstition that finally we lose sight of its essence.

Spiritual Mind Treatment

Our use of the science of mind we have called by many different names, and intentionally so. We did not desire that the new ideas advanced be in any way limited by previous meanings that might becloud their significance. Prayer, creative thinking, meditation, positive thinking, affirmation, and any and all other terms or expressions one might use—let us take them all and include them in the larger expression: spiritual mind treatment. We use the term *spiritual* mind treatment rather than Christian mind treatment, or Jewish, or Hindu, or any other kind of mind treatment. We use the word spiritual as we would use the word beauty: beauty which is the essence of the beautiful. It applies to every race, every creed; it applies just as effectively for a pagan as for a Christian. We happen to be mostly Christians by background and culture, but this has nothing to do with spiritual mind treatment either as a spiritual fact or as an active scientific law.

Spiritual mindedness is a persistent and consistent attempt to feel the Divine everywhere and in all things. It is the capacity not only to believe in but also to perceive, to feel, and to react to a unitary wholeness—an essence, an infinite personalness, a beauty, a love, and a joy, which exists in the universe—the Divine Presence. Spirituality is normal, natural, spontaneous, effervescent, never studied or labored. David Seabury, well-known psychologist and author, in writing on the subject of metaphysics and prayer said, "If we seek guidance for what we are doing in the physical world from the great Wisdom that exists in the invisible Universe, we are simply uniting the various parts of our world so that it becomes for us one with the Universe."

Spiritual mind treatment, then, means exactly what it says— that the One Mind reacting on, in, through, and as the body and environment will change a situation because we change our thinking within It. ". . . Be ye transformed by the renewing of your mind. . . ." As we increase our awareness of Spirit, Its nature is more fully expressed in our lives. As we change our thinking there will be a change in our body or the body of our affairs.

Philosophy, science, and religion have said time and time again that mind and matter are the same thing; in one aspect

Mind is intangible matter and in another aspect it is tangible as form. This corresponds to Einstein's famous formula stating that energy and mass are equal and interchangeable. It does not say that energy energizes mass; it says it may become mass. Therefore in spiritual mind treatment we deal with the concept that there is no difference between the *essence of form* and the *essence in form,* because the essence of form, in form, *is* form. We need to remember that we do not deny our mind or our body, but that we do affirm Spirit, which encompasses them both. We add to but do not take from.

The Basis of Spiritual Mind Treatment

Our whole endeavor is based on an understanding that *mind in essence* and *mind in form* are one and the same thing. In other words, we are not trying to reach a known fact with an unknown or unknowable principle. We are not spiritualizing matter or materializing Spirit to heal a disease or a condition. There is no such thing as a spiritual control of a material universe as though Spirit were separate from it, for Spirit and matter are not opposites but a fundamental unity.

Most important to remember is that there is no God supervising a human kingdom, and there is no law of nature higher than another law of nature. Nature is not in conflict with itself. Nature is One System; God is One; Existence is One. Therefore spiritual mind treatment deals with disease, or any undesirable experience, not as an unreality in experience but as a wrong arrangement of things, largely the result of man's own thought. And thought, rightly arranged, will automatically rearrange the conditions on the basis that Mind and matter are equal and interchangeable.

Our whole approach to spiritual mind treatment is very simple: The Universe in which we live is at Its foundation a conscious intelligent spiritual system operating through and as Law—the Law of Mind in Action.

Proper Attitudes

The spiritual mind treatment we give will not be complete until we are attuned to the Infinite. It will not be complete until we get a clearance from a sense of rejection and guilt; therefore we will have to forgive ourselves and others. In addition we must come to realize intellectually and emotionally that there is nothing in the Universe to be afraid of. There is no fundamental evil, there is no duality. Whenever consciousness perceives the transcendence of spiritual Reality it almost automatically sloughs off all other things.

There is a rhythm in the Universe, which rightly understood would resolve all conflict. There is a peace in the Universe, a freedom from confusion, which rightly understood would heal all troubles. There is an all-encompassing love in the Universe, which rightly understood would heal all emotional difficulties. There is a creativity in the Universe, which rightly understood would keep us whole and vitally active in expressing it.

In our use of spiritual mind treatment we must always keep in mind the fact that the higher form of intelligence governs the lower. That everything below the threshold of consciousness is subject to the level of awareness to which our consciousness has grown. Everything less than conscious intelligence is a form of unconscious intelligence which functions either on the pattern inherent within it or impressed into it by the individual mind or the race mind, the collective unconscious which Jung so convincingly demonstrated.

As we proceed in the use of spiritual mind treatment we find that there is no difference between the thought and what it is going to do. What it is going to do is announced by the definiteness of the thought, the nature of the declaration, but the doing and the ability to do are not that of the thinker. This cannot be overemphasized. This means that the individual does not do the healing of the body, the condition or situation, but that if he did not use spiritual mind treatment the result might not be accomplished. He does not inject himself into the situation as the factor that does the "doing," but rather what he does is to consciously use a natural energy, intelligence, and creativity at the level of his consciousness, his recognition and feeling of it. In this sense he becomes a spiritual scientist, one who uses the science of mind.

The Technique of Designing

What then is the technique of spiritual mind treatment? The formation of words to conform with an idea—an idea, of course, that harms no one—and with a conviction that they are true and that nothing in our mind rejects what we say; then, identifying what we say with the person, place, or thing we desire to change for the better. That is all there is to it! It is simplicity itself!

In effective spiritual mind treatment we need to speak from the heart, yet at the same time what we say must in no way be in conflict with the intellect, but instead be supported and upheld by it.

The use of spiritual mind treatment of necessity is based on the idea that there is an intelligent Law in the universe which receives the impress of our thoughts as we think them and acts upon them without question, without argument, without rationality. It creates for us in our experience the content of our thought with mathematical accuracy. This is the Law of Mind. To the degree we understand our unity with Spirit, or God, and give to the Law only ideas of good, we expand our thought and free ourselves from the negative consequences of our previous limited thinking.

The Declaration

The technique of application, the manner of our declaration, is very clear. Suppose we are giving a spiritual mind treatment for John Doe. Following the initial steps of recognition and identification with the Power greater than we are, we might proceed something like this: "This word I speak, this treatment, is for John Doe. He lives at 124 North Street in Chicago. There is only God's perfect pattern, perfect idea of him, and that is his life now. This is the spiritual truth about him, therefore all that appears opposite to it is eliminated from his experience." Or we might say, " 'Every plant, which my heavenly Father hath not planted, shall be rooted up' and cast out of his experience."

These are but statements to convince the mind of the person giving the treatment; any statement which will bring conviction is good. No two treatments can ever be alike lest we should listen to ourselves speak; and we must not listen to what we say but to what we really think and feel, because our speech so often affirms what we should not listen to. We need to let the simple child of faith within us counsel the man of experience, that the man of experience shall find out what is good and seek to follow it.

No Formulas

There is no prescribed formula for a spiritual mind treatment because every time we give a treatment we must expect it to be the only time we are going to give that one. It must always be a new and spontaneous formation. The moment it becomes mechanical it loses much of its effectiveness and power. A technique may be correct but the feeling and temperament are not always in it. It is always out of the fire of the heart that the mouth must speak. Therefore do not wonder what words you should use. Treatment is spontaneous, the manifestation is mechanical. Treatment follows a Law of Intelligence and its objective manifestation corresponds to our conviction and use of that Law.

Unlimited Applications

There is no difference between the use of spiritual mind

treatment for the healing of a physical condition and its use for the correction of a situation in our affairs or for a greater supply of abundance of any good thing. Each act is purely a process of thought. We reduce a condition to a mental concept and then correct what needs correcting in that mental concept. We do not deny the reality of things as they are, but raise our thought, our consciousness, to a level of a greater perception and acceptance of the spiritual Source of all substance and supply, and declare that out of It our desired good is manifest in our experience now.

We know that thoughts have the ability to create new experiences and conditions. In the case of the person who is alone and lonely we may arrive at the conviction that "there is no limitation in Spirit, and no limitation in this person's life for he is one with Spirit and he now has new experiences, he meets new people, encounters new things, enjoys new situations." As this is done we are setting in motion for him the Law of Mind which operates on all things, spiritual, mental, and physical, and sooner or later he will meet a whole new set of circumstances. We must always remember that out of the impulsion of our thought there is a compulsion, that a creativity is set in motion which has prerogative and initiative. As the impulsion of our thought is lifted to a higher level of understanding something new must evolve.

It is our privilege, our obligation, to create for ourselves a new design for living. Every time we think, something new is being done. God is not a static God and there is no time when creation begins; in the eternal *now* Spirit moves upon the face of the waters. In the eternal *now*, by thought, Spirit moves as the Law of the Universe and out of it arises a new creation.

Generalizations

Although it is very important to be definite and specific in spiritual mind treatment, we may also initiate a new chain of causation just by affirming that something new and good is going to happen. In many instances it is beyond our ability to know or to fully comprehend what needs to be done or what action should be taken. We may at the moment have no mental equivalent of the particular good that is necessary to fulfill a need. In such a case the need will be fulfilled because our mental equivalent rested in our ability to expect and to receive something. We often make a mistake if we think that we must have an exact mental equivalent of *every* experience.

The Ability Is Everyone's

Always remember this, no matter what we are giving a spiritual mind treatment for, whether it pertains to ourselves, other people, or conditions, we first find out what is wrong, then know that the opposite thought will erase it. Start as simply as that. Everyone can do it. No one can think any better than another, and no one has any more authority about it; no one is any closer to God than another. The one who is willing to abandon himself to the Genius of the Universe, to the realization of his intimate relationship to It, and who applies his thought and feeling and all that he is to this conviction, will find not a void but a solid foundation for the creation and experience of a joyous new life, a new life that is the outward manifestation of a new pattern of thought.

BASIC RULES

In all of our endeavor to create a better life, whether it be in regard to health, affairs, or relationships, we must keep foremost in our minds these salient points:

1. We are living in a spiritual Universe. There is one creative Source of all things. God, Mind, Intelligence. It is both the Creator and the creation.
2. Law is impersonal. Law is the way or medium by which thoughts

become things. It is the way God becomes His creation. Our thought is creative through or by means of the action of Law.

3. God is personal to each one of us. God is what we are, is in us as us. Our mind, part of the One Mind, is creative of good in our experience at the level of our understanding of the nature of God.

In the practical use of our thought in everyday living through spiritual mind treatment we need to remember the four vital elements involved in the application of the science of mind so as to make it a dynamic and directive command unto that for which it is spoken:

1. Recognition of the Power greater than we are.
2. Conscious identification of ourselves with It.
3. The specific declaration of our word, backed by complete intellectual and emotional conviction.
4. Acceptance of the word we have declared as being a spiritual reality right now, and that as such it will of necessity have to be manifest in our experience. And in our acceptance there must be an expression of thanks, a feeling of gratitude that it is now so.

23 PRACTICAL SUGGESTIONS

. . . If ye have faith as a grain of mustard seed, ye shall say unto this mountain, Remove hence to yonder place: and it shall remove; and nothing shall be impossible to you.

—MATTHEW 17:20

THERE MAY BE many who will ask: How is it done? How does one give a spiritual mind treatment? And, probably, rightly so. But it must always be remembered that *how* it is done depends on the individual doing it. And even more important, the right *way* of doing it can only be determined by the person himself in and through the doing and the results achieved. Nothing will happen, there will be no results, no effects, unless there is the *doing*. If we want results we must act so as to insure that there will be results.

Most people find it valuable and effective to devote a specific time each morning and evening for constructive work, but no one time is any better than another. Actually one should continuously maintain an attitude and frame of mind that embodies the essence of a spiritual mind treatment.

As for the place, it does not matter. One should be comfortable, quiet, and free from interruptions and distractions. Although some may be able to think clearly and specifically for a period of time in hectic surroundings, we mostly seem to need a place of quiet and solitude.

As for the length of time that should be devoted to a spiritual mind treatment, this is also an individual matter. Depending on the person and problem being dealt with, the time may vary from one or two minutes to thirty or more minutes. The deciding factor is: how long does it take to make a declaration of the good desired, to *become convinced*, to accept intellectually and emotionally, that it is so? Many have found that it is advantageous to make their treatment work oral, to actually speak the words. This often makes more specific many ideas which otherwise would be very nebulous.

The whole process of giving a spiritual mind treatment is a relaxed, effortless endeavor. Just as there is no strain, no pressure, no forcing of things in the enjoyment of a beautiful sunset, there should be only a complete absorption in and the focusing of attention on the desired good during the giving of a treatment.

Now that we have determined a place, a time, and a proper attitude, we are ready to make practical use of the four steps, the four elements, which should be included in a spiritual mind treatment. These we found were: Recognition, Identification, Declaration, and Acceptance. In the following illustration of a spiritual mind treatment it must be remembered that the words it contains are creative only to the extent one is able to give them value and meaning. It must also be remembered that what is said here is but an illustration of a technique; each individual will have to devise his own effective way of thinking creatively.

You must enter into every period of treatment with a complete conviction that the word you speak is instantaneously and perfectly manifested, that it is the creative pronouncement of the One Mind through you, at the level of your awareness, and as such it bears the fruit of its own action.

You may start out in this way with a *Recognition* of a Power greater than you are:

I know that there is One Presence, One Power, One Life, One
Intelligence, One Substance. It is perfect, whole, complete,
and harmonious. It is the source of all things and is in and
through all things. There is nothing separate from It. There is
nothing that can limit Its action, there is nothing that can be
separate from Its action. It always knows what to do, how to do
it, and when to do it. It is the limitless source of every good
thing. It is all joy, all happiness, love, harmony, and perfection
in all that It is and does.

The next step is one of *Identification,* one of relating yourself to Life—God:

There is One Life, that Life is God, that Life is perfect, that
Life is my life, *now.* There is nothing in me or in my experience separate from God. "I am that which Thou art, Thou art
that which I am." What I am is God in me as me. I now rid
my mind of any and all ideas of isolation and separation from
God, and know that as I now turn to Him I permit and partake of an increased flow and influx of the Divine nature as
what I am. I am one with God—all that is. My mind is a focal
point, an individualization, of the Mind of God, the One
Creative Power. The word I speak, the declaration I make is
the word of God going forth through me into new tangible
creation. In accord with the Law of Mind my word is its own
fulfillment.

In proceeding to the next step, that of the *Declaration,* it is
always necessary to keep in mind that you are not asking or
begging for anything. You are declaring something as true,
affirming the reality of the good you desire. In other words, it
is a demand you are making upon the Universe, which according to Its nature has no choice other than to fulfill the demand
according to the nature of the demand. You are not seeking
to make God, Life, other than what It is, but are instead claiming your good out of Its infinite potentialities.

This word I speak is for me, about me, is the truth of me.
There is nothing in my mind, or the mind of another, that can

deny it. Its action and fulfillment cannot be delayed, deferred, or hindered. I know, affirm, and declare that Divine Intelligence, the Mind of God, now guides and directs my every thought, my every action. I know what to do, when to do it, and how to do it. Every good idea I have carries with it the knowledge of the ways and means for its achievement. I am vigorous and whole. I possess the vitality of the Infinite. I am strong and well. God's Life is my life, now. His strength is my strength. His power is my power. My whole being is renewed, invigorated, made alive. There is peace, a Divine harmonious, dynamic, creative action at the center of my being. Every breath I draw, every beat of my heart, is the perfect rhythmic action of Life Itself. The expression of the One Perfect Life in me as me is now perfectly maintaining every atom, cell, and organ of my body. My body is a Divine idea in the Mind of God and no thing, no situation or condition can prevent Its full and complete expression in and as me. God created my body, knows how to maintain it, to remove what doesn't belong, and to rebuild it. This is occurring right now. Without reservation I know I now manifest and experience in all fullness and completeness God's perfect idea of me, and in all respects, every action, function, and structure of my body now conforms to it. There is perfect assimilation, circulation, and elimination. All that I am is one with the One Perfect Life. All the joy there is, all the happiness, all the beauty are now mine. I am born of the Spirit. I am in the Spirit. I am the Spirit made manifest.

Many find it very valuable at this point to deny those ideas which may contradict the statements that have been made. To declare that they are powerless, noncreative, and ineffective. In such cases the denial should be followed by affirming the opposite; there is a removal of a negative and it is replaced with a positive idea.

All that you do, or can do, in making a declaration is to convince yourself. You reach a point where nothing in your thought denies your faith, belief, and conviction in the truth and reality of the ideas you have expressed. The declaration you make is nothing more or less than a statement of what you believe God to be, and what you believe yourself to be, for you are within what God is, which is perfect.

The final step is that of *Acceptance*. The gift is always given, and but awaits our acceptance of it. All that is is ever available, this we may know and affirm, but there needs to be the taking, the accepting. And we must always do the accepting *now*. Not an hour from now, or tomorrow. The Universe only acts now, so there must be the immediate acceptance of our declaration as a spiritual Reality, as a Divine cause now active.

I now accept the creative action of the words I have spoken as the law and the thing whereunto they are directed. They go forth into immediate fulfillment. Right now are they fully manifest. There is no delay, there is nothing that can prevent them from now being fully and completely fulfilled in my experience. They are words of power and of good. I accept them, I know they are the truth of that which I am. In and through them God goes forth anew into creation. It is now done, it is now complete. For this knowledge, for this understanding, I am grateful. I give thanks that all this is so. I know and accept that there is One Life, that Life is God, that Life is perfect, and that Life is my life now. Right now. And so it is.

Many people find that after they have finished giving a spiritual mind treatment they want to stay quiet for a while. They seem to have a relaxed feeling, a deep sense of gratitude and an inner thanksgiving and joy, in which they desire to remain for a time.

On the other, if this is not your feeling, if you begin to wonder if the spiritual mind treatment you have given will be effective, such wondering is a denial of everything you have said. You have said that you *know* the words you have spoken are true. If you have done your work right there will be nothing in your thought or feeling that can in any way question the truth of your statements.

In instances where you give a spiritual mind treatment for

another you use his or her name instead of saying that the words you speak are for yourself.

It is of course realized that the example of a declaration just given is not necessarily very specific in respect to particular problems or situations which you may desire to have corrected. You will have to work out such statements for yourself. However, a few suggestions for dealing with certain problems are given here and numerous others will be found in the Appendix.

RIGHT ACTION

Everything that I think, say, or do is governed by Divine Intelligence and inspired by Divine Wisdom. I am guided into right action. I have confidence in myself because I have confidence in God. I am sure of myself because I am sure of God. I am aware of my partnership with the Infinite. I know that everything I do shall prosper.

HAPPINESS

Every thought of not being wanted, or of being afraid; every thought of uncertainty and doubt is cast out of my mind. I rely on God alone, in whom I live, move, and have my being. A sense of peace and certainty flows through me. I am surrounded with friendship, love, and beauty. Enthusiasm, joy, vitality, and inspiration are in everything I do. I accept complete happiness, abundant health, and increasing prosperity. I have confidence in myself because I have confidence in God. I am sure of myself because I am sure of God.

PROBLEMS

The Spirit within me knows the answer to the problem which confronts me. I know that the answer is here and now. It is within my own mind because God is right where I am. I now turn from the problem to Spirit, accepting the answer. In calm confidence, in perfect trust, in abiding faith, and with complete peace I let go of the problem and receive the answer.

SUCCESS

I know exactly what to do in every situation. Every idea necessary to successful living is brought to my attention. The doorway to ever-increasing opportunities for self-expression is open before me. I am continually meeting new and larger experiences. Every day brings some greater good. Every day brings more blessings and greater self-expression. There is no deferment, no delay, no obstruction or obstacle to impede the progress of successful action in my affairs. I am prospered in everything I do.

ABUNDANCE

I identify myself with abundance. I surrender all fear and doubt; I let go of all uncertainty. I know there is no lack of any good thing in my experience for the Presence of God is within me. The freedom of God is my freedom and I now cease dwelling on limitation and give my earnest attention to the particular abundance I desire. The Abundance of God fills my good desire right now.

LOVE

Today I bestow the essence of love upon everything. Everyone I meet shall be lovely to me. My soul meets the soul of the Universe in everyone. This love is a healing power touching everything into wholeness.

SECURITY

The Law of Good is flowing through me. I am one with the rhythm of Life. There is nothing to be afraid of. There is nothing to be uncertain about. God is over all, in all, and through all. God is right where I am. I am at peace with the world in which I live. I am at home with the Divine Spirit in which I am immersed.

CONCLUSION

It is hoped that your journey through the pages of this book has been a joy and a pleasure, and that you now have a new evaluation of yourself, the world you live in, and the Power that is greater than you are.

As for designing a new life for yourself, you are now on your own. This might be a good time to remind you: *If at first you don't succeed, think, think again.* It can be done, and you can do it. Thousands of people around the world are proving to themselves and to those about them the fact that the ideas you have encountered do work, and the life they are living is a dramatic testimony to their validity.

As for the ideas presented there is nothing new about them. They have been advanced during the ages, as well as today. They are the pronouncements of those who have had the courage to think and to follow their thoughts to a sensible and logical conclusion. What may be new here is the approach to these ideas and the way in which they can be used in a practical down-to-earth manner in everyday living.

The great adventure lies ahead of you. Discover within yourself that Divine spark which may be fanned into a glowing flame, giving you warmth and security. The light from it can certainly and surely guide you to the greatest experience any man can have—the experience of the Presence of God to whom and through whose Law all things are possible.

May you go with God.

APPENDIX

For those who may desire to continue the designing they have started, there will be a desire, no doubt, for other suggestions relative to spiritual mind treatments.

On the following pages are numerous ideas on a great many subjects that may be of value and assistance. They cover situations and conditions that most frequently seem to need correcting in the course of everyday living.

Some are presented in the form of a meditation followed by a specific declaration or affirmation. Others are simple declarations for inclusion in a spiritual mind treatment.

Remember that these are suggestions. Only you can give them, in your own words, and through your own depth of feeling, the vital, dynamic, creative quality necessary for them to be effectively manifest in your experience.

The time will come when you will need nothing outside yourself. When in the sanctity of your own thought you will be able to find your way alone, alone with God, to a fuller experience of all the good that Life holds.

LIVING TODAY

It is known that it is not the particular negative experiences through which we have gone in the past that need destroy our happiness, but rather it is our emotional reaction to those experiences carried in the reservoir of memory. Many people suffer complete defeat without having really been defeated, others succumb the first time anything goes wrong. It is one of the aims of psychosomatic medicine, analytical psychology, and psychiatry to strain out the negative mental and emotional reactions to previous experiences. Our experiences are stored in the mind either as happy or disconsolate ones, as life-giving or morbid. There is just as real an infection of the mind as there is an infection of the body. Almost invariably our negative reactions to life, our unhappiness, and perhaps most of our physical disorders are based on unhappy experiences which are buried, but buried alive, in our memory. But they can have no real existence of their own in today other than as lengthened shadows. And so it is that as the impulsions of yesterday are carried over into today, making today happy or disconsolate, so the reactions of today are creating the possibilities of tomorrow, prophetic of what we shall experience.

Yesterday is gone, tomorrow has not arrived, but today I am living in an eternal present filled with an everlasting good. There is nothing unhappy or morbid that can remain in my consciousness. I no longer have any fear of yesterday nor do I anticipate tomorrow with anything other than enthusiastic expectation. Everything that was good in yesterday shall perpetuate itself in my experience. Everything good in today shall create my future. Therefore I have no fear either in looking forward or backward but realize the eternal day in which I now live. In this day there is no fear, no lack, no want, no doubt, no misunderstanding, no uncertainty. Today is big with hope fulfilled, with love and life well lived. Tomorrow will provide its own blessings.

ACCEPTANCE

Spiritual mind treatment really is something we do to ourselves. The only direction we give to this treatment, this prayer, this affirmation of acceptance, is that we identify it with the person we are working for or the condition we wish to help. This is neither willing, concentrating, coercing, nor compelling anything or anyone. It is, rather, a quiet inward acceptance, an affirmation of our conviction, based on the theory—which to us is a certainty—that there is a spiritual Perfection at the center of all things in the universe, and that there is a fundamental Law of Good governing all things. There is One Life, that Life is God, that Life is our life now. Consciously we identify ourselves with that Life, definitely we affirm the One Presence and the One Power operating in, around, and through us. We should believe that everything that denies the supremacy of the Divine Presence and the Law of Good is itself but a mistake in judgment. Strangely enough and unbelievable as it may sound, this rather lofty attitude of thought, which seems so far removed from the realities of human experience, is accepted by every scientific mind in the world. There is no scientist who believes that there is anything that can contradict, refute, or hold sway against a principle that is established.

Today I accept my own affirmations. There is nothing in me that can contradict them. I have a deep inward sense, a feeling and conviction and complete faith that there is a Law of Good governing everything, and that It is governing completely, with absolute certainty, without deviation, with no exception; that there is nothing to oppose It, nothing to change It, nothing to limit or circumscribe Its action. I abandon myself to this faith. I live in its atmosphere and accept its conclusion. I know that I am a Divine being on the pathway of an endless self-expression and that the Eternal God is my host, now and forevermore.

IDENTIFICATION

Spiritual mind treatment is an affirmation of the Divine Presence in and through all things, all people, and all events. God is one as a Divine Presence, and there is one intelligent Law governing all things. We live in this Divine Presence and may consciously use this universal Law. But someone might ask: How does our prayer, our treatment, or our affirmation reach the person, the place, or the thing we wish to help? This question both simplifies and answers itself when we come to realize that there is but One Spirit, One Law, and One Presence, and that we all are identified in this One Life, not as being separate from It but as individualized expressions of It. Since this is true, whenever we identify our thinking with some person, place, or thing, we identify them as the object of that thinking, and automatically, because there is but One Law or Intelligence operating, the result of that thinking will be for that person, place, or thing. Since the person, place, or thing we are treating or praying for (as some term it) is in the One Mind, the One Spirit, and the One Law, then the mere act of identifying him or it with our affirmation causes the reaction of that affirmation to appear.

Today I am identifying myself, everyone else, and everything I do with the Divine Presence. I am not trying to influence people, I am not holding thoughts to make things happen, I am not concentrating Divine energies for any purpose whatsoever. Rather, I am still, knowing that God is over all, in all, and through all. Through my affirmation I am watching, expecting, and knowing that there will be a reaction through whatever I identify with my word. Therefore I am at ease, I am relaxed, I am at peace, and I am filled with a feeling of enthusiastic conviction. Today I realize what is meant by the saying, "Before they call I will answer." And I am identifying everything in my life with an answer that affirms the Divine Presence and the Law of Good—right action, happiness, success, prosperity, and well-being for everyone.

POWER OF THE WORD

In treatment we are dealing with a Law of consciousness and a Power greater than we are. But every power in the universe is greater than we are, every law with which we deal is something that we could not reproduce. We may only use it. The slightest fact in nature is a miracle that we cannot perform, and it is an intelligent person who does not feel embarrassed if he cannot explain everything in life. We have to start with the self-evident proposition that there is a spiritual truth that makes us free; that there is a way to use It; that we may rely upon it; that it will not fail us. We must come not only to believe and accept, but also permanently to know that there is a Power greater than we are, and we can use it. Then as we affirm that we are one with the living Spirit, that God is all there is and there is nothing else, our word, being the presence and the power and the activity of that Spirit, is the Law of Good and it cannot fail to operate. Let us feel that there is something permanent about the word we have spoken. Just as we plant a seed and walk away from it and nature takes it up and the law of its own being evolves it, so let us believe the same thing about our word of identification with Good— something takes it up, something evolves it as our experience, it will manifest.

"So shall my word be that goeth forth out of my mouth. . . ." I affirm that it is the word of God establishing harmony in my experience. With utmost simplicity I accept my own affirmation and believe in the answer to my own prayer because it is a prayer of acceptance. There is an Intelligence, a Power, and a Divine Presence operating in and through my life, guiding, directing, governing, bringing good to pass in my experience. This affirmation of acceptance endlessly repeats itself in my experience, for whatever I identify my word with is lifted up in consciousness to the level of my acceptance.

Divine Patterns

There is a Divine pattern for man, and each of us is an individualization of it. We become consciously unified with the pattern or the spiritual cause back of things by lifting our thought above the confusion of everything that has seemed to separate us from good. In psychosomatic medicine and all other forms of psychological adjustment, the suggestion of a universal pattern back of things, a pattern which in itself and of itself must be perfect, is automatically being dealt with. It is no idle statement to affirm the perfection of God at the center of all things, manifesting in and through each and every thing in a unique way. We should spend more time meditating upon the harmony, the beauty, the peace, and the joy that must exist at the center of our being, something that is unconfused and whole. We cannot believe that this wholeness was created by us or ever came into being through a process of evolution. Quite the reverse. All evolution is a result of the action of an imprisoned splendor which exists at the center of our being.

Today I seek the Divine pattern at the center of my own being. Affirming its reality, I permit its essence to flow through me. Claiming it as my very own, I embrace it. Believing in its beauty, I sense its harmony. Accepting its peace, I am calm. Living in its love, I am unified with life. Believing in its power, with childlike faith I accept the authority of its action in my everyday affairs. And looking at the God in man, I see in everyone the pattern of His perfection, the image of His likeness, and the joy of His being.

RELAXATION IN TREATMENT

If we feel that our thought, by our own will and through the power of concentration, must go out somewhere into the invisible and compel things to happen, then we shall put strain into our prayer or treatment. Someone may exclaim: But I don't see how thought works. And he would not be alone— no one sees how it can become our experience. This is the way it is with all the laws of nature. All we understand about them is that they *are*, and we know a little about the way they work. So it is with the law of faith and belief or affirmative prayer, which we call a spiritual mind treatment—something greater than we are acts upon us. If we had the same faith in spiritual laws that we have in physical ones then our faith would be complete and miracles would happen every day just because there is something acting upon our thoughts. As we turn to the Divine center within us, then, realizing the Presence and the Power and the Activity of the living Spirit, let us announce that our word *is* the activity of the Law of Good; without effort, or strain, and in a relaxed acceptance, let us permit this to be so, not asking how or why, but, with simple acceptance and complete belief.

Accepting that the Law of Good is right where I am, I announce the Presence and the Activity of this Law in all my affairs, knowing that they are governed by Divine Intelligence. Today everything in my life comes under the control of this Intelligence. Everything is harmonized by It and unified with It. Consequently, I completely accept Divine guidance. I know that I shall be guided in everything I think, say, and do, and I know that peace and joy and happiness shall flow from me to everyone I meet. Today everything in my experience is made glad, and joy goes before me making every experience happy and radiant with life.

AFFIRMATION AND DENIAL

By far the larger part of our thinking processes are automatic, casting, as it were, the images of our acceptances into the universal Law of Mind which reacts upon them. And thus it is that fear can bring about the condition feared while faith can reverse it. In spiritual mind treatment, affirmation and denial is for the purpose of erasing the wrong thought patterns and establishing correct ones. This practice is both scientific and effective in that a denial tends to erase the negative conviction while an opposite affirmation tends to establish a new thought pattern which works as automatically as the negative one did. This affirmation can either instantly or gradually establish an inward recognition which becomes permanent. The whole theory of affirmation and denial in spiritual mind treatment is built upon an understanding that the Law of Mind itself accepts the meaning and feeling of the words which we utter as though they were true. The Law of Mind is like a mirror. Therefore the treatment must bring out evidence that causes our whole inward being to accept the affirmation which we make of good, substance, supply, health, happiness, or success. If you practice this method and watch the result of this simple process you will discover that an idea logically presented to Law will produce a definite result.

Today I affirm the All-Good and in this affirmation I deny that there is any presence or power of real evil in the Universe. I affirm the presence of love and repudiate every belief that hate has any power. I affirm peace and deny confusion. I affirm joy and declare that sadness has no place in my consciousness. I affirm that God is over all, in all, and through all. There is nothing out of the past that can limit me and there is nothing in me that can limit my future.

PHYSICAL PERFECTION

When we speak of physical perfection we are not saying that no one is sick or no one has pain. We are merely implying that of necessity there must be, and is, an essence of Perfection at the center of everything, including the physical body, and that Perfection must exist now whether or not we know it. If that which is whole within itself were not already here neither medicine, psychology, nor affirmative prayer could in any way benefit us physically. For whatever the medication or manipulation or emotional adjustment or prayer of affirmation may do, it does not and cannot create life, it may only reveal it. This every physician and surgeon knows; this every intelligent psychiatrist accepts; and this you and I affirm. This is what we mean when we say that every organ, action, and function of our physical body is rooted in a Divine Life and in this Divine Life there is no congestion, no wrong action; there is always perfect circulation, assimilation, and elimination. Through such statements we are trying to sense the greater Reality. Believing as we do in all of the healing arts that help mankind, and being grateful for them and cooperating with them, we do in our practice definitely affirm that toward which they and we all reach—the spiritual perfection of things.

I affirm that my body is a body of right ideas, for it is the creation of God. Every organ, action, and function of it is in harmony. Whatever does not belong to my body is eliminated. Whatever does not belong is being removed continuously. All the energy and all the action and power and vitality there is in the Universe is flowing through this Divine creation now. My body is established in the action of that harmony which eternally exists. There is One Life—perfect, harmonious, whole, complete. That Life is my life now—not yesterday or tomorrow, but today.

PERSONALITY

Would it be too much to say that personality is the use or misuse we are making of a unique *something* which is expressing through it? Would it be too much to say that back of every personality there must be a Divine pattern of individualization which we but dimly perceive and even more inaccurately interpret? If so, our personality has a possibility far beyond anything that is merely physiological or psychological; it has the possibility of becoming not a mask to hide the reality behind it, but an open countenance through which this individuality becomes expressed. It is true that there are many personalities but each is only some reflected form of *that* behind it which is greater, and which may flow through the individual personality expressing warmth and color and love, unity and peace, joy and happiness. We should learn to sense this greater Self. There is a pattern of God behind every personality, an individuality seeking unique expression through it, and to this we should surrender everything that we are, for this surrender will not cause us to withdraw from life; it is not an escape but a revelation, and an instrumentation of something greater than we appear to be.

Today I express myself, believing that there is a Presence hidden within me which is both the Reality of my true being and the Presence of God. I consciously unite my personal self and all of its actions with this over-dwelling and indwelling Reality. I know that the vitality of the living Spirit flows through my personality, invigorating it. I know that all of the warmth and color and beauty that is there pours through it. I do not deny my personality, rather I affirm that all of its impulsions and actions flow from a greater Source, the true Reality of the living Self, the Presence of God in me as what I am; and does reveal to me the same Reality in others, the same exalted Divinity manifesting Itself through the innumerable faces of humanity.

SUPPLY AND ABUNDANCE

Spiritual science cannot promise something for nothing. It does not teach that you can have anything you want, no matter what it is, or that your thought can precipitate a million dollars. It does, however, teach, and it can demonstrate, that a betterment of circumstances and conditions and relationships can be brought about through spiritual mind treatment, which means an inward realization of the action of a Power greater than you are in your affairs. It would be unthinkable to believe that the creative Intelligence of the Universe could lack anything, or that It could plan for Its creation to lack that which expresses Its own being. We may be certain that the Divine intends only good, only abundance for Its creation because It is the very essence of life and givingness. In spiritual mind treatment for success, for right action, and for right compensation, we work to know that Divine Abundance is forever flowing into everything we do. We are guided by a Divine Intelligence and impelled to act on this guidance. In other words, we do not expect someone suddenly to thrust a fortune upon us, but we have every right to expect that we shall be gradually led from where we may be to something better and more abundant. Anyone who will give spiritual mind treatments over a period of time will be able to prove this.

Divine Abundance is forever manifesting Itself in my affairs. I desire to do only that which is good and constructive, life-giving and life-expressing. Therefore I know that I shall prosper in everything I do. I know that I exist in limitless possibility, and that the infinite Good is right where I am and active in my experience. I believe that everything for complete self-expression is now the law of my individual being. New thoughts, new ideas, new situations are forever unfolding before me. There are new opportunities for self-expression and for abundant life and love and happiness. This I expect, and this I accept.

RICHER LIVING

Why should we go through life as though it were something that had to be endured? As though there were not enough good or joy to go around? Are we not always limiting the possibility of love or affection, of appreciation, and of the common everyday good things of life? If we really are in union with a Divine Source, then there should come a feeling of abundance in everything we do—an abundance of friendship,

an abundance of self-expression, an abundance of everything—
for the more abundant life contains all things whether we call
them big or little. It is a sense of this more abundant life that
we should acquire, a feeling of the urge of that which is greater
back of everything we do, a sense of the flow into our consciousness of the Divine Intelligence, a feeling that the creative
imagination of the whole Universe is centered in our creative
act and flowing through it. We should consciously practice
this more abundant life, not only for any specific thing or
good we desire, but for the realization of the All-Good flowing
through everything and everyone. Should we properly attune
our consciousness to this Divine Abundance, automatically we
should find a betterment in everything we do, a broader and
deeper experience, a higher realization, and a greater good.

Today I expect the more abundant life by keeping my every
thought and expectation open to new experiences, to happier
events, to a more complete self-expression. Giving out more
love, I know a greater love in return. Sharing with life whatever good things I have, I know life shares with me the good
that it possesses. Seeing beauty everywhere, I have a revelation
of still more beauty. Seeing joy in everything, I know genuine
laughter. More deeply sensing the Divine Tranquillity in which
all things exist, I have a deeper consciousness of peace and
security. Through it all I know that I am in the embrace of a
warm, loving Presence forever seeking an outlet through me.

RESULTS

Today I affirm the action of the Law of God. Today I accept
the result of my own affirmation. I ask no one for any justi-
fication of my conviction. Boldly I proclaim the Divine Presence and humbly and with complete conviction I accept the
revelation of that Presence in every avenue of my life. This
conviction in the integrity of my own soul I proclaim, with
no fear of opposition. Alone with God and the Law of Good, I

make my claims upon the Infinite, the Divine hidden in everything, the dynamic Law of creativeness, existent in all things.

MONEY

All supply is of Spirit and money represents a form of my supply. Money is a Divine idea. It flows to and from me, enabling me to be comfortable, prosperous, and to enjoy the pleasures of life; God withholds no good thing from me. The Mind which created me now stimulates my thought and effort into greater right activity. I am not in bondage to money; instead, money now serves me as I serve life. Money is a symbol of God's Abundance, and I accept that which is rightfully mine.

EXPECTANCY

Today I go forth in joy, knowing that everyone is my friend, knowing that I am a friend to all people. I believe that Divine Love protects me and Divine Intelligence guides me. It is my sincere desire to share everything I have with others and to expect for them the greatest good which I hope for myself. In this way life becomes a communion of Spirit with Spirit. Knowing that the same Spirit, the One Spirit of the living God, is in all, over all, and through all, I believe in and accept a good greater than I have ever experienced.

GOOD

Today I affirm the supremacy of Good and everything within me responds to this thought, understands its meaning, and announces its presence. There is a Power greater than I am flowing through me into everything I do or think about, automatically making everything right. There is a Transcendence coordinating, unifying, causing all the experiences of my life to blend into Its unity, into Its oneness, and proclaiming the power of Its might. As a child accepts life without question, and love without argument, and action without anxiety, so do I spontaneously accept the operation of a Power greater than I am as the Divine Governor of everything I do, the Divine Provider of all my needs, the Divine Presence diffused through all my thinking.

LOVE

Today my love goes out to all people and all things. There is no fear in this love, for perfect love casts out all fear. There is no doubt in this love, for faith penetrates all doubt and reveals a unity at the center of everything that embraces all things. This love flowing through me harmonizes everything in my experience, brings joy and gladness to everything, brings a sense of security and well-being to everyone. And I realize that the love flowing through, in, and around me and all things is one vast all-enveloping Love forever emanating from the living God.

FORGIVENESS

Today I forgive everyone and accept forgiveness by everyone. I know the eternal Spirit harbors no malice toward me or anyone else. Forgiving and being forgiven, I have an inward sense of peace and tranquillity. There is no anxiety, no sense of guilt, no fear of judgment. All mistakes of the past are now wiped out in my consciousness and I no longer carry any burden from them. I look forward to the future with joy, in peace and gladness, and live in the present day with an inner assurance of being one with all life.

I AM MYSELF

Today I practice being my real self. In so doing I do not deny others the same privilege, but seek to find in them the same miracle of life, the same wonder of being, the same delight in existence. Today I realize that all the Good there is, all the Presence there is, all the Power there is, is immediately available and immediately responsive to me. Today I enter into the faith of believing, the joy of knowing, and the act of living which proclaim the One Power and Presence in all things. And today, as a child, I accept this Presence that responds to me as warm, personal, and colorful. It is within and around and through me even as It embraces all things. Today I accept my partnership with the Infinite.

SELF-EXPRESSION

Today I express myself with joy and enthusiasm. I live more abundantly and I accept the possibility and the responsibility. I look more deeply into the heart of all people finding there the pulsation of the Heart of the Universe Itself. I penetrate all externals and reveal the Divine Presence hidden there, the Presence of the living God. And I know in this my self-seeking, this my self-expression of the abundance of the Whole, there is nothing little or mean, there is nothing isolated or separate from the All-Good. This Good is to me even as It is to others. As I lift high the chalice of my hope and faith I know that it shall overflow, that everything I do shall be blessed, every good I seek shall be expressed through me, and everyone I meet shall proclaim anew to me that God, the living Presence, is expressing Himself through all humanity and rejoicing in that which He does.

HEART

Today my heart beats in perfect rhythm, and its tireless and effortless pulsations are steady, calm, and continuous. God created it and I now permit God to sustain its perfect action. I cease burdening its action with fear, violent emotions, anxiety, and doubt; and I accept the wisdom, love, and harmonious activity of God in my body and affairs. The perfect action of the One Life is manifesting in my heart right now.

SUCCESS

I know that I am a creation of God and have my existence in and am maintained by Him. In God there are no failures; there is nothing that can prevent God from succeeding. I now permit God's Action to express fully through me. I meet with success for I now accept completion of my every good undertaking. My success is the success of God.

STOMACH

My stomach is created by Divine Intelligence as the perfect organ of digestion. This Wisdom sustains and maintains its every action and function. No food, thought, or emotion now interferes with the ease and comfort of its activity, for I now accept the harmonious expression of God in me, which keeps my stomach renewed and the process of digestion perfect.

EMPLOYMENT

There is the right position for me, now, and I accept the activity of God which places me in it. Nothing can hinder the creative action of the One Mind in and through me and all necessary channels open up for it to be properly expressed. "I have a wonderful work in a wonderful way, and I give wonderful service for wonderful pay." For all this, in deep gratitude, I do give thanks.

GOD WITHIN

Since there is but One Life present everywhere, I must be in that Life and of It, and It must flow through me. It must be what I am, therefore I accept this Omnipresence as something real, definite, immediate. At the very center of my own being I realize the Divine Presence. At the center of my own consciousness I recognize a transcendent Principle forever renewing my being; a Divine Presence forever animating, sustaining, vitalizing, re-creating; a Divine Consciousness forever guiding, directing, inspiring. There is within me that which knows what to do and compels me to act in accord with its perfect Law and Order, and its complete Peace. This I accept, and even as I affirm it I know that this Omnipresence is alive and awake and aware within me.

WEIGHT

I know that there is, right now, the balanced activity of the One Life in my body. All food is used properly, and that idea which may have caused me to eat too much or too little is now relinquished. Weight needed is added; all excess weight is discarded. The Wisdom which created my body now sustains it in all ways as I, without reservation, now continually accept Its perfect action.

FEAR

I know I cannot be apart from God. Created in His image and likeness, I am established in His Life and surrounded by His Good. Past mistakes no longer rob me of today's happiness, and I know the future holds only the promise of a more complete expression of the God-self within. Fear is no part of that which is All-Good and I release it gladly. I let my confidence be in the Good which flows from God. This I now claim and know is mine.

WHOLENESS

God does not give Himself in part; nothing of Good has ever been withheld from me. I dwell in Wholeness and have access to all that may illumine my mind, maintain my body, and rightly govern my affairs. My spirit is the Spirit of God in me which gives me the use of a Power that brings my thought into form. I now let my thought be of the Wholeness of God and confidently accept Its manifestation with thanksgiving.

Suggestions for Further Reading

For those who desire to pursue further the ideas brought forth in this book, the following reading material is suggested:

HOLMES, ERNEST. *The Science of Mind.* New York: Dodd, Mead & Company, 1950.
  The classic writing in the field of modern metaphysics. It is known and used around the world as a guide and authoritative text for spiritual mind treatment.
KINNEAR, WILLIS H. (ed.). *The Creative Power of Mind.* Englewood Cliffs, N.J.: Prentice-Hall, Inc., 1957.
  In this volume are brought together the ideas of more than fifty of the greatest minds of our day, from the fields of science, philosophy, and religion, explaining the creative nature of our minds and the way to use it.
Science of Mind Magazine, 3251 West Sixth Street, Los Angeles 5, California.
  The outstanding monthly magazine in its field. Established in 1928, its circulation is now world wide. It unites current thinking in science, philosophy, and religion in a universal "science of mind" for everyday living. World-famous authorities in all fields are represented. It also contains a spiritual mind treatment for each day of the month.

INDEX